TRADITION AND CONTRACT

THE LEWIS HENRY MORGAN LECTURES/1973
presented at
The University of Rochester
Rochester, New York

TRADITION AND CONTRACT

The Problem of Order

Elizabeth Colson
University of California, Berkeley

ALDINE PUBLISHING COMPANY, Chicago

ABOUT THE AUTHOR

Elizabeth Colson is Professor of Anthropology at the University of California at Berkeley. She received a B.A. and M.A. in Anthropology at the University of Minnesota, and an M.A. in Anthropology and a Ph.D. in Social Anthropology at Radcliffe College. Her experience in field research spans more than thirty years, and she has had research and teaching assignments at Harvard University, Rhodes-Livingston Institute, Manchester University, Boston University, Brandeis University, the Center for Advanced Study in the Behavioral Sciences, and the California Institute of Technology. Professor Colson has written more than 100 reviews, articles and sections of books, and is the author or editor of numerous books including *The Makah, The Plateau Tonga, The Social Consequences of Resettlement,* and *Autobiographies of Three Pomo Women.*

First published 1974 by
Aldine Publishing Company
529 South Wabash Avenue
Chicago, Illinois 60605

ISBN 0-202-01131-3 clothbound edition
Library of Congress Catalog Number 74-82603
Printed in the United States of America

CONTENTS

FOREWORD	vii
ACKNOWLEDGEMENTS	ix
1. AN EXPLANATORY INTRODUCTION	1
2. LEWIS HENRY MORGAN AND THE STUDY OF POLITICAL SYSTEMS	9
Morgan and the Social Contract	10
Morgan's Influence on Political Anthropology	13
Morgan and the League of the Iroquois	19
3. A SOCIETY OF EQUALS: THE PROBLEM OF CONSENSUS	31
Constraint and Reciprocity	35
Standards and Consensus	51
4. THE LIMITS OF AUTHORITY: KNOWING THE RULES	61
Liberty and Authority	62
The Useful Court	69
Controls on Power: Tradition and Legality	74

5. THE SEARCH FOR UTOPIA 89
The Perfectibility of Men 92
A New Social Order: Utopian Dreams 96
The New Social World 102

REFERENCES 115

INDEX 127

FOREWORD

Since their inauguration in 1963, the Lewis Henry Morgan Lectures have annually provided stimulation for those who have attended them, and each of the published series has found an interested and receptive audience.[1] The Lectures not only commemorate Morgan and his work; they have as additional aims the encouragement of exploration and the presentation of recently developed views in anthropology.

Professor Colson's Lectures, which opened the series' second decade, pay full attention to all these aims. Her intention, expressed in her title and in her text, is to consider "the problem of order," a matter of concern to Lewis Henry Morgan, a host of later anthropologists, and innumerable others in diverse fields.

Readers of these Lectures will find carefully forged links with the work of Morgan and that of others. They will also discover

---

[1] The connection of Lewis Henry Morgan with the University of Rochester, and the initiation of the Morgan Lectures in 1963, are briefly discussed in the Foreword to Professor Meyer Fortes' *Kinship and the Social Order* (Aldine, 1969).

that Professor Colson's skillful use of material from her work during the past thirty years with the Plateau and Gwembe Tonga of Zambia contributes, in a unique way, to the structure of her argument and to illumination of her major theoretical points.

As has been customary at the time of the Morgan Lectures, Professor Colson provided much additional stimulation, beyond her formal presentations, in seminars and spontaneous discussion. Readers of the Lectures will be able to appreciate her ability to clarify difficult theoretical issues in a highly original way, helpful to faculty and students alike.

The 1973 Lewis Henry Morgan Lectures were delivered on April 3 to 12, and this volume is a revised version of them.

ALFRED HARRIS
Department of Anthropology
University of Rochester

ACKNOWLEDGEMENTS

In writing this book, I have drawn heavily on the ethnographic literature and on work in political anthropology. Though this is not a monograph based on field work devoted to a particular people, I have drawn on my own experience, more especially on research among Plateau and Gwembe Tonga of Zambia. This experience now spans almost thirty years. My debt to Pomo, Makah, and Tonga teachers is obvious. I also owe a particular debt to Dr. Thayer Scudder, of the California Institute of Technology. For eighteen years we have collaborated in a long-term study of Gwembe Tonga. Each of us has had complete access to data collected by the other. Over the years we have also traded ideas as we discussed the data so that it would now be difficult in many instances to assign one or the other of us as the source for a particular idea or interpretation. Nevertheless, any use I have made of the data on the Gwembe Tonga or any interpretation I may have made here about the nature of Tonga society is my responsibility. Dr. Scudder has not had the opportunity to read this manuscript. Support of our research in

Zambia came originally from the Rhodes-Livingstone Institute, now the Institute for African Studies in the University of Zambia. In later years the Institute continued to provide a base and logistic support, but after 1963 research costs were provided by other agencies. I have had a grant from the Joint Committee on Africa of the Social Science Research Council and the American Council for Learned Societies. Our field research in 1972 and 1973 was supported by Grant No. GS-3295, National Science Foundation, made to us jointly through the California Institute of Technology. Dr. Scudder has revisited Zambia on several occasions under the auspices of the Food and Agricultural Organization of the United Nations. The National Institute of Mental Health (Small Grants Division), the California Institute of Technology, and the Committee on Research of the University of California, Berkeley, have provided funds to support the analysis of Gwembe data. The latter supported the typing of the manuscript by Carlyle Rispoli.

My other debts were incurred directly in the writing of this book. First, I must thank the University of Rochester for inviting me to give the Lewis Henry Morgan Lectures and so providing the occasion for this book. The original lectures owed much to the critical comment of Dr. Penelope Hartland-Thunberg. Those who heard them delivered at the University of Rochester in April, 1973, raised queries that influenced my reworking of the argument. The substance of Chapters One and Two was presented at a dinner meeting of the social anthropologists at Berkeley in October, 1973. My colleagues at Berkeley, Dr. Burton Benedict and Dr. William Shack, read the lectures in manuscript. I have benefited greatly from their comments, some of which are incorporated into this final draft.

Bibliographical citations of most of the publications referred to in the text follow the usual convention but some classical works in political philosophy and Lewis Henry Morgan's own books are cited by title. This is because I have consulted them in recent paperback editions. I used *League of the Iroquois* (1851) and *Ancient Society* (1877) in the most recent editions, edited by William Fenton (1962) and Eleanor Leacock (1963). All who turn to Lewis Henry Morgan as a continuing stimulus to the reexamination of the nature of social life or for a vision of Iroquois society owe a special debt to their editorships and to the introductions and notes they contributed to the new editions.

TRADITION AND CONTRACT

one

AN EXPLANATORY INTRODUCTION

When the invitation came to give the Lewis Henry Morgan Lectures for 1973, we were at the end of the 1960s. The universities had known a long period of turmoil: most of the traditional rules had been questioned, many ideas of hierarchy and structure had been under attack, and many students and some faculty had demanded that academic life be based upon contractual agreements rather than implicit assumptions. We had also heard much about a generation disillusioned with the old order, both within and outside the universities, and about why that order should be replaced by the creation of free-form associations based upon consensus arrived at through constant negotiations. Some were already experimenting with alternative communities; these for the most part dissolved almost as quickly as they formed even though they were based upon ideals of consensus and negotiation and the belief that people should be free to do as they would. Behind many of the experiments seemed to be a vision of some kind of extended family unit or small face-to-face community lacking formal offices. Their advocates seemed to have given little or no thought either to the context within which the different units or their members could find means of arbitrating differences or to devices for controlling expectations or activities that promised to disrupt the general community.

These are matters to which anthropologists, including myself, have given much thought. I have spent much of my professional life trying to understand how people cope with each other in the absence of formal government, as members of the kind of societies we sometimes call stateless, but which Lucy Mair (1962: 61, 78) has suggested we might better see as subject to minimal or diffuse government. The questioning going on around me led me to think more intensively about the nature of legitimacy and authority and about what it is that holds social groups together in long-term association.

Like Lewis Henry Morgan, I had my initial training on the nature of such societies from American Indians. The Pomo, of California, and the Makah, of Washington, had once lived in small settlements composed of households, each with a great deal of autonomy. Each settlement, if not each household, could be regarded as an independent self-governing polity. They claimed to have recognized no political offices with jurisdiction over the whole settlement, although the various ritual offices associated with secret societies might be said to have had political functions. Informants also claimed that they had recognized no hierarchy of command beyond the household even though they had had a clear appreciation of differences in rank and wealth. By the time I came to talk with Pomo and Makah at the end of the 1930's, the days of their independence were far in the past; they were by this time either members of a reservation society subject to the Bureau of Indian Affairs or were living on small rancherias which came under the mandate of the sheriff's office and a variety of county and state officials. Nevertheless, they looked back to a past when, as one Makah woman said, "It seemed like a law was just what they did in those big families."

Later, in Central Africa, I found myself among first the Plateau and then among the Gwembe or Valley Tonga of what was then Northern Rhodesia and was later to become Zambia. By the mid-nineteen-forties, Tonga-speakers must have numbered about 300,000. Even in the nineteenth century they had far outnumbered the Pomo, the Makah, or for that matter the Iroquois in their heyday. But they too had lived in small neighborhoods which had once been the largest territorial units that could be called self-governing polities, although ties of kinship and bond friendship, as well as a system of clanship, connected their residents with other Tonga-speakers and indeed with people speaking other languages. And again, as with the Pomo and the Makah, the Tonga, by the time I first met them in 1946, had been drawn into a political system characterized by an administrative hierarchy and other highly developed governmental institutions. Older Tonga, however, had reached maturity in the days before colonial rule and knew life in communities where, as they said, "Any man might call himself a chief, but that did not mean that we would follow him." If their social order was not an anarchy in its lack of formal leadership positions through which law could be promulgated and enforced, then it met all the conditions which Rousseau had claimed necessary if a participatory democracy were to work. Even at the present time, though disciplined by decades of exposure to appointed chiefs and to councils and courts imposed upon them from above, as well as by a district administration with its messengers who exerted police power, the Tonga still have little respect for hierarchy. Instead, they stress personal independence, the equality of all men, and the right of each man to make his own law. Indeed, I have heard them maintain that they are not bound by any decision to which they have not been a direct party.

The Tonga in particular have taught me something about

what it means to live without the formal apparatus of courts, police, or public officials. Some of the devices they used, and still attempt to use, for organizing and regulating their affairs are recogizable as common to other small-scale communities that must depend upon persuasion and stalling tactics for social control. Indeed, some of these devices are not unknown to the academic world and the world of committees with which I sometimes deal, if survival and continuity come to be more important than individual interests or adherence to abstract principles.

Anthropologists since Lewis Henry Morgan have specialized in the kind of face-to-face egalitarian societies that some would have us create. In the last century, since the publication of *Ancient Society* (1877), we have carried out research among their members, argued about their nature, come up with alternative models of their organization, and been influenced in our diagnosis of the basic tasks they face by our own particular views of the nature of humanity. It is this that emboldened me to choose a well-worn topic, which might be phrased as "the advantages and disadvantages of living under authority." Political philosophers have dealt with it from the time of Aristotle, and no doubt before that. But let it be said in my own defense, I do not propose to trace yet once again the origin of the state or to examine again the bases of its power. I do propose to argue that social life involves controls, applied by ourselves, by our peers, or by those who in some way have acquired the power to judge our actions and to act upon judgment. We may be free to negotiate with our fellows about a great many things, but one thing we are not free to negotiate and that is freedom to do as we will. I shall be concerned with the kinds of limits people set upon their own freedom of action, as well as with the devices they attempt to use to protect such freedom as they have from encroachment from above and to control those who claim authority over them.

In the next chapter, I shall begin, as is only appropriate, with an assessment of Lewis Henry Morgan's contribution to political anthropology and to the study of systems of social control; Morgan, and his contemporary Sir Henry Maine, are founding fathers of social anthropology. Morgan pioneered the study of the regulation of public affairs in the absence of rulers, hierarchies of office and a chain of command, attributes we usually assume when we speak of government. His work is therefore directly relevant to a consideration of the nature of order. I propose first to discuss Morgan's assumptions about the basis of government, then examine his impact upon the development of political anthropology, and finally, because like other anthropologists Morgan was dominated by the vision given him by his ethnographic experience, I shall turn more closely to his description of the Iroquois political order. This provided him with his type model for societies without a developed executive. Morgan's questions about such societies differ from those we would ask today when we have come to concentrate not so much on political units and political institutions as upon the purposes for which men create and maintain boundaries and the ways in which they use their institutions in the on-going thrust of involvement with their fellows. Given Morgan's interest in clan-based polities, it is perhaps easiest to show the changing focus in anthropology by contrasting his view of clanship with my own, derived primarily from experience with clanship in Central Africa.

In the third chapter I shall focus more specifically upon both the constraints faced by people living in societies without centralized governments and the role of consensus in the maintenance of order. Small face-to-face communities share several attributes: 1) dense social networks, and 2) an expectation of continuity of relationships with the same people over time. As we shall see in Chapters Three and Five, these have important consequences. Gluckman has called such societies "multiplex," emphasizing that each individual plays not one but a variety of roles in interacting with each of his fellows: a fact that encourages both a certain consistency in behavior and the use of methods of social control centering on the crucial importance of reputation. Small face-to-face communities are likely also to have two other characteristics: 1) a *de facto* similarity in life style for those within the same community, and 2) a similarity in organizational principles (structure) common to the various communities which exist within the same social field. This last has been most clearly demonstrated by the socio-linguists and by the structuralists led by Levi-Strauss. In this third chapter, however, I shall not be concerned with formal institutions but rather with the purposes for which people mobilize the forces of social control and the devices they use to create consensus and implement a decision.

The fourth chapter will deal with the role of tradition and legality in controlling superordinate authority. Put in another way, it is the use of rules to control the rulers, as people become drawn into large-scale social orders controlled by centralized governments with specialized governmental institutions. In this chapter I shall argue that individuals who know the disadvantages as well as the advantages of the small-scale unit and the limitation of minimal or diffuse governmental institutions have seen the possibility of a greater security in an incorporation into larger units with administrative structures. They may not have welcomed colonial rule, but, when it first appeared, not all saw in it an unmitigated disaster. Once engulfed in the new form of organization, however, they find themselves subject to very different risks. It is no longer enough to restrain themselves to avoid embroilment with neighbors. They have now both to avoid behavior that will embroil them with authority and to find ways to escape the demands that reforming or encroaching officials make upon them.

The fifth and final chapter will be devoted to a discussion of contemporary developments, largely within Central and East Africa, where people are facing the common problems of the twentieth century. These include: 1) the growth of cities where anonymity creates an opportunity, for those who see the advantage of using violence in gaining their ends, to escape from the controls either of neighbors or of specialized offices; 2) the appropriation of the power of centralized states by bureaucracies who apparently assume that government is an end in itself; and 3) the realization that new opportunities and rapid social and geographical mobility raise bruising questions about conformity and consequently, about the persistence of traditional styles.

African leaders of newly independent states meet head on the questions of legitimacy, consensus, and power bases as they try to build a new order. Intellectuals and average citizens alike try to find new social categories useful for defining how members of formerly discrete units who are now joined together as a common citizenry are to behave. Or to put it more succinctly, people need to know who they are in relation to each other and therefore require sets of roles defining who does what in relation to whom. Political leaders are rewriting the laws governing the distribution of rights and privileges. They change legal institutions in the hope that a single system of courts operating with specified procedures and definitions will handle disputes between citizens throughout the country and so underline the fact that they are all one before the law. Like many others who succeed in gaining power, African leaders are less aware of the need to find a means whereby citizens can pursue grievances against the state and its agents.

The political leaders who came to power in the 1950s and early 1960s were committed to the belief that men have the right to join together to challenge governments that do not represent their interests. They were then firm upholders of the theory of the "Social Contract," though they followed Locke and Rousseau, rather than Hobbes, in believing that governments that failed to improve the common lot and uphold common liberties had violated the contract and should be deposed. Today's rulers are more likely to refer to an African tradition of respect for authority and to the right of the government to make demands upon its citizens in the building of a new order.

African leaders deal with Utopian blueprints, but sketch very different Utopias from those shown on the blueprints of egalitarian communes or the constantly bargaining small polities put forward by student activists of the 1960s. They also cope with the realities of power politics and, in a determination to stay in power, make compromises with ideals they still enunciate.

While they plan and try to govern, citizens who were once members of small parochial units move about the country more freely than ever before. Whatever their prejudices are against those from other sections of the country, these citizens are having to come to grips with their common membership within a single economy and polity. They must find some way of identifying those they meet so as to define how they shall deal with each other. Their new social categories then are created as a means of coping with existing realities rather than as part of an overall plan or in response to political ideologies. As they use common facilities, compete for the same prizes, and respond to the same governmental actions, they become a common citizenry with all that this means in terms of common and conflicting interests. They do not build Utopias and are uncommitted to a single dream. But they do hope to find in government the means whereby they can have justice and security from violence. They look to it moreover to provide schools and medical services and to ensure the economic growth that will provide the jobs through which they hope to obtain the material things the Western world now takes for granted. Whatever their quarrels with government, they want good government rather than less government.

two

LEWIS HENRY MORGAN AND THE STUDY OF POLITICAL SYSTEMS

Morgan's political theory rested upon the assumption that men developed their social orders through conscious thought and rational choice. His vision of the social process appears to be one of free men, and sometimes women, assembled together for the discussion of public affairs. Resek, his biographer, comments that Morgan had no idea "that democratic political theory rested on the complex reflections of a Locke or a Jefferson" and that he "never paid much attention to the history of ideas because he was certain that since the dawn of creation men, indeed all animals, were guided by plain reason" (Resek, 1960: 18).

Though Morgan may have paid little attention to the history of ideas, it would be cavalier to follow his example and dismiss his own contribution. This chapter therefore is devoted to a consideration of how Morgan viewed the development of political institutions and the way in which his general theory reflected the very particular Iroquois experience.

Morgan and the Social Contract

I have found no reference in either *League of the Iroquois* or *Ancient Society* to the work of Locke or Bentham, but Morgan surely was one with them in spirit when he stressed that government was a covenant or contract among free men. Some writers have tried to distinguish between covenants and contracts. They define covenants as agreements resting on moral rather than legal obligations and enforcible by religious sanctions rather than by courts; contracts, on the other hand, specify relationships spelled out in legal terms and therefore are subject to litigation and enforcement by courts and political officers (Firth, 1936; Shack, 1963). Morgan, however, saw *all* agreements as ultimately resting on the right of the public to exercise choice, and so, theoretically at least, subject to adjudication.

If government rested upon a covenant, it found its appropriate expression in the representative council whose development Morgan was concerned to trace from its beginnings in the council of the clan through the assemblies of Greece and Rome to the legislative bodies of the United States. Like any good upstate New Yorker of his generation, Morgan was prone to view the United States as the direct heir of the golden age of Greece and of Republican Rome (Resek, 1960: 15–16). Monarchy—or any arrangement that emphasized the executive office at the expense of the ultimate authority of the representative assembly—he regarded as an usurpation and an unnatural perversion of the normal progression of governmental institutions created by men as they worked their way from "savagery to civilization."

Now I know that many passages in *Ancient Society* can be quoted to show that Morgan believed in historical determinism or that he accepted an organic model of society. He, after all, was writing for his contemporaries and used the terminology acceptable to them, a terminology based upon a biological model. He sometimes spoke of change being initiated through "unconscious reformatory movements to extricate society from existing evils" (*Ancient Society,* p. 58). More frequently he ascribed change to the deliberate reformatory actions of particular individuals, who acted of their own initiative although their scope for innovation may have been restricted by what Morgan calls "the slow accumulation of experimental knowledge" (*Ancient Society*, p. 3). In fact, Morgan regarded societies, nations and states as units created by men for their own purposes, much as he and his friends in Aurora, New York, had created "The Grand Order of the Iroquois" (Resek, 1960: 16, 23). His own history gave him instances of men entering into solemn compact with one another in the Mayflower Compact, the Continental Congress, and then in the federation of the United States of America. The Iroquois assured him that they had done the same thing when they founded their Confederacy and that they had recommended to the colonists that they follow the Iroquois example in creating a union. Stern (1931: 164) has noted that both *Systems of Consanguinity* and *Ancient Society* "are permeated" with the belief that societies change because of "designed reforms."

His own contemporaries recognized the importance Morgan gave to rational choice and criticized him for it. This is at the heart of much of the criticism McLennan and Lubbock leveled at his work (Stern, 1931: 164). It also helped to alienate Morgan from Sir Henry Maine and Sir Edward Tylor, who were primarily responsible for creating the concepts used by the British anthropologists of the following generation who in turn pioneered the next intensive examination of a diversity of political regimes. Maine and Tylor emphasized the importance of custom, the role of tradition, and the primacy of religion over legislation in giving legitimacy to law (Feaver, 1969: 32, 46,

49, 57). Morgan's emphasis upon rational choice alienated him also from Franz Boas, who both founded academic training in anthropology in the United States and introduced the German concept of culture, derived from Herder, Hegel, and the German romantic tradition, making this the master concept of American anthropology. This emphasis of Morgan's also differentiated him from Durkheim and his followers, whose assumption that men act before they think and then produce a conceptual order to explain what they have done, has been so influential. The anthropological traditions initiated by these men, especially by Boas and Durkheim, drew upon a European experience foreign to Morgan. He could link upstate New York to the Iroquois and to the classical periods of Greece and Rome, but not to feudal Europe or the intellectual ferment associated with the end of the feudal order and the rise of nationalism.

Morgan, then, wrote from an intellectual tradition derived from Locke. This tradition rested upon the theory of the social contract and stated that governments were created by contract *and* were bound by the contract that created them.

Morgan was confirmed in his assumption that governmental forms were created by rational choice when he came to know Eli Parker and other Iroquois. These men and women described to him the nature of their former political system and attributed its origins to an agreement to form a league for the purpose of outlawing vengeance and regulating relationships among the member nations, for the purpose of securing peace, as well as enabling them to "resist the pressure of contiguous nations."

Government for Morgan therefore rested upon the consent of the governed, who had chosen the forms under which they would live. For him the problem of legitimacy had been solved. It is noteworthy that whereas Morgan accepted the Iroquois at their word and interpreted the origin of the League as due to a "constitutional convention," Anthony Wallace, one of the foremost students of Iroquois history in our own day, instead attributes the founding of the League to a revitalization movement based upon a visionary experience of Hiawatha. According to Wallace, Hiawatha used the charisma of that experience to convince his fellow Iroquois that the new dispensation he preached was supernaturally sanctioned and therefore had authority over them (Wallace, 1958; 1970: 97–98).

Both agree, however, that the new creation was a success and that it created the framework for peace within the League based on a respect for the rights of its people, associated with a policy of violence towards all who refused to accept its domination.

Morgan's Influence on Political Anthropology

The social contract was not congenial to the anthropologists who succeeded Morgan either in America or Europe. Morgan's failure to dominate the development of political anthropology must be attributed, in part at least, to the fact that he wrote from a theory of government which had already been explored by earlier political thinkers and was under attack by contemporaries who were attempting to understand why the new orders so rationally planned by revolutionary leaders did not achieve their purposes. But there are other reasons why his study of political systems was less influential than his study of kinship. In kinship studies, Morgan had no real predecessors and few contemporaries. His demonstration that radically different methods of classifying kin exist was a challenge to current assumptions about the nature of man: in the jargon of today, he initiated a paradigm change and provided the basic intellectual tools required for developing the new paradigm. But while men of his day may have thought that the kinship classification they had learned as children was a universal human phenomenon, they had no such illusions about their governments. His description of segmentary political systems, therefore, did not have the impact of his work on classificatory kinship systems.

You will notice that I have been freely using the terms "government" and "political" as though these had accepted definitions in anthropology. They do not. Morgan granted government to all societies so long as they were composed of corporate groups which could enter into relationships with each other, regardless of whether or not they recognized any form of executive. On the other hand, he believed that political life was found only within what he called the state, whose appearance he attributed to a developed technology that allowed for the appearance of wide differences in wealth and of classes with specialized interests. Since the publication of *African Political Systems* in 1940 (Fortes and Evans-Pritchard), social anthropologists have been less certain that government is everywhere in existence, but they have agreed with Aristotle that man is a political animal. This still permits them to quarrel about the definition of "political" and to bring down upon themselves the strictures of the political scientists. Radcliffe-Brown (1940: xiv, xviii) provided a definition which placed the emphasis on "the maintenance or establishment of social order, within a territorial framework" and confounded political structure with "the rule of law." His definition was predicated on the assumption that men live in communities and that each and every community has the same primary public policy—the control of violence. This necessarily involves each community in the provision of some means for the adjudication of disputes. For him the hallmark of the political was agreement. For Edmund Leach, who did a great deal to change our perspective and reverse our priorities with the publication of *Political Systems of Highland Burma* in 1954, the hallmark is competition, and the search for supporters. Recently he has said, "A man is engaged in *political* action whenever he behaves in such a way as to rally others to support a cause in which he is interested" (Leach, 1973: 29).

Those who emphasize competition are likely to speak of political fields, arenas, resources, and strategies (Swartz, Turner, and Tuden, 1966, pp. 271–279, Bailey, 1968, 1969), rather than of political communities under a rule of law. A political field is not a moral community, nor are those affected by it necessarily bound by a law to which they have given consent. Some of us find it difficult to accept the ultimate implications of a definition of political behavior that appears to substitute personal ambition for an acknowledgement of a public good; it implies that might makes right and that success justifies the means. We are inclined to agree with Marc Swartz and his colleagues who insist that any definition of the political must include both a public and public goals, and that competition related to these goals ultimately must be refereed by the public (Swartz, Turner, and Tuden, 1966: 4–5).

"Political" implies to me that people are organized in relation to some kind of public goal. "Government" appears to be best defined as the means whereby people are constrained or constrain themselves. My use of the term "state" derives more from *African Political Systems* than from *Ancient Society,* since rule through an organized executive with a hierarchy of offices seems to me a more crucial variable than the appearance of social classes. When the organization of public affairs is left either to the community as a whole or to specialized categories who hold a collective office, I shall follow Mair in speaking of them as having minimal or diffuse governments.

Morgan, as I have already said, pioneered the study of societies with diffuse or minimal government. When he wrote *League of the Iroquois,* he sought to understand the Iroquois mode of government by resorting to Aristotle and Montesquieu. By the time he wrote *Ancient Society,* he had adopted the ethnographer's stance and tried to understand other societies in terms of the Iroquois model. Where once he perhaps chided the Iroquois for not conforming to the rules laid down by the masters, he now was certain that the masters must be wrong if what they wrote contradicted his Iroquois model. Unfortunately, he was not content to see Iroquois as a variant of a generalized type, but rather expected to find the specific characteristics of Iroquois clans and council in all societies that lacked the technological development to underwrite the appearance of classes and a highly institutionalized governmental structure.

However much Morgan's writing stimulated Marx and Engels or other social evolutionists, his ethnographic specificity created difficulties for anthropologists who were also ethnographers. The specific features of his model would have been of very real utility to anthropologists trying to understand and describe the organization of Indians living in the eastern United States, but most of these Indians were already exterminated or in exile in the west by the time the next generation of American anthropologists appeared. Morgan's insistence on the primacy of unilineal descent groups and popular assemblies meant that his model had little utility for Boas who was trying to understand the Central Eskimo and the Kwakiutl, just as later it only served to bewilder me when I tried to understand the bilateral descent groups that provided the basic units of Makah society. His model was also of little use to Robert Lowie working among Plains Indians who emphasized men's associations rather than clanship as the basis of governing units. Morgan's eclipse as a political theorist among American anthropologists is therefore easy to understand. It is also true, of course, that for a number of reasons they showed little interest in the study of political systems until the 1950s. By then the field was dominated by concepts derived from field work in Africa, where a sufficiently large body of data had been collected to allow for a greater degree of abstraction and therefore a broader applicability than Morgan could have achieved from his Iroquois work and the scanty ethnographic record of his day.

The Africanists might have found an inspiration in Morgan, who shared with them an interest in social systems, social instituttons, and social units, but the particular social institutions and social units he had emphasized were not of immedate interest to them. Maine, Durkheim, and Radcliffe-Brown were to be more influential in providing the models used by the Africanists for describing the kinds of political systems they were encountering.

Morgan's emphasis upon clan and council also did him a disservice, even though some of the ethnographers worked in areas where clans and councils did in fact exist. Morgan had regarded clans as antithetical to monarchy, aristocracy, or theocracy; in many African regions, however, members of clans also lived in kingdoms with rulers holding extensive powers.

Morgan furthermore had regarded monarchy as a usurpation and late deviation from what he regarded as the true line of governmental development which led through various stages of the representative assembly—to Morgan the ultimate legitimate governmental institution. This meant he had little to say about monarchies, a major kind of polity discussed in *African Political Systems,* whose appearance in 1940 marked the first major statement by anthropologists on comparative political institutions since Lowie's *The Origin of the State* (1927). Although Morgan had a good deal to say about segmentary political systems, which were of even greater interest to ethnographers working in Africa, his particular model did not fit the segmentary lineage systems whose complexities were to hold the stage for the next decade.

Given the colonial milieu, writers for *African Political Systems* may well have underplayed the importance of assemblies and councils, for the colonial system emphasized the executive at the expense of other aspects of government. Councils that may once have shared power with monarchs or provided the principal means of government had been downgraded to become either courts of law or ritual adjuncts to kingship. Legislation and the formulation of new solutions to emergent problems had to be carried out largely under the guise of an affirmation of old traditions and was done by the courts, as described in Chapter Four. Neither judicial nor religious attributes of government had been of much concern to Morgan who emphasized rather the creation of consensus through free discussion and the struggle for the control of policy between the council and the executives it appointed. It is only in very recent years that action within councils has begun to receive any very concentrated attention by ethnographers of political power, and they have not felt the need to go back to Morgan for their inspiration (Bailey, 1965; Richards and Kuper, 1971).

In the mid-1950s, anthropological theory began to deal with strategy rather than structures. It focused on embattled actors and actions rather than on the development of institutions. The new approach was engendered by exposure to situations where rapid change seemed to be the order of the day. Assumptions based on bounded political units and legal communities governed by law did not appear to be particularly useful in understanding or describing what was happening. It was more helpful to talk in terms of political fields, in which men manipulated wealth or other advantages to extend their spheres of influence and their control over their fellows. Constraints on action were attributed to ecological and technological factors rather than to institutionalized rules. Theoretical models based on experiences in Highland Burma, the entrepreneurial activities of the "Big Men" of Melanesia and New Guinea, and the party politics of India and Africa replaced earlier models which had assumed stability and the sanctity of established orders. Although their proponents might have agreed with Morgan that men exercise choice and can create new institutions, they differed from him on a fundamental question. That is, they assumed that those involved in political action were seeking to enhance their own power rather than involved in a search for the general good. In a sense, they were proponents of a blind evolutionary force, for a better system can arise only by chance combination rather than through rational planning.

The belief that the political process is a repetitive struggle between factions, from which men are rescued only by chance or some external force, shares a basic pessimism with Wallace's assumption that reform can be carried out only by a charismatic movement based upon a religious revelation (Wallace, 1958). Morgan's more optimistic approach may be more congenial to a new generation of anthropologists, but this remains to be seen. Whether or not they share his optimism, however, they would find in him the seeds of a theory of alliance, an arguable theory of the basis of government, and a model of one form of segmentary society. These are not negligible achievements.

Morgan developed his theory in conjunction with his work on Iroquois society. It was this perspective that gave him his special vision. The remainder of this chapter, therefore, examines more specifically how his understanding of the Iroquois illuminates certain problems we face in developing working models of the way men order their affairs, create categories which permit them to interact with one another, and limit themselves by their own decisions.

Morgan and the League of the Iroquois

Morgan was fortunate in the fact that the society he sought to understand was radically different from those on which much earlier political theory had been built. The Iroquois conceptualized their political order as an alliance of matrilineal descent groups, which today we would call clans. The Iroquois were also somewhat exceptional in that they not only held to matrilineal descent but also to matrilocal residence.

Frequent wars also affected their system. Military campaigns that took the men away from home for months and sometimes years at a time, had thrown much of the responsibility for the maintenance of society upon the women, who, in staying home, ensured the food supply, ran the household, and developed a considerable esprit de corps, enabling them to control a great deal of what went on. They decided marriages and exchanged men to ensure a system of alliances between households; senior matrons chose male representatives to sit in local and confederacy councils.

In addition, constant warfare had given other power to women, power not officially recognized in Iroquois ideology. They *were* the Iroquois, while the men were frequently enough recruited from outside. Men lost to their households and clans through warfare were replaced with aliens, adopted by clan matrons who chose thereby to save particular captives from death under conditions of excruciating torture. Apparently they also had the right to reverse their decision, though presumably as time passed it would become more and more difficult to do so. Nevertheless, a large number of men were on approval, not only in the household groups of their wives, but within the wider Iroquois society itself. The official councils were composed of men, who received great respect in their role as council members, but they were present as representatives of communities of women, who were their matrilineal kinswomen, real or adoptive, rather than their wives and children. If their constituents found them unsatisfactory, a recall was more than a theoretical possibility.

Striking contrasts are what make the anthropologist recognize and come to terms with his own assumptions. It seemed reasonable enough for those whose vision of early man was conditioned by biblical sources or classical accounts of the Greek or Roman family to conclude that government had its origin in the patriarchal family and the authority of the father. The latter was then the forerunner of a king whose power ultimately was vested in patriarchal power and the sanctity of the father. The use of kinship terms and the family analogy in European political discourse made it easier for them to come to this conclusion, although I rather suspect that both usages were late in development. When reading William Chaney's *The Cult of Kingship in Anglo-Saxon England* (1970), I was struck by the frequency with which the early documents he cited referred to the king as "the good shepherd" and the absence of the patriarchal image. Regicide did not appear to be equated with patricide. The first use of the metaphor "the king is in the position of a father" was dated 1028 A.D. But this is an aside which I shall not pursue.

Morgan, with the Iroquois example in front of him, could not confuse the family with the political unit. He defined the family, as we still do, as a unit composed of husband, wife, and children. He was well aware that the Iroquois father played no role comparable to that of king or ruler in the household unit where lived his wife and children. He could not find in the family the origin of either the matrilineal clan organization or the larger political units in which the clans were associated. Morgan was vehement on this point and generalized from the Iroquois data to a proposition that clans did not arise from family organization and that political power was not the "father writ large." Something other than piety had to be invoked if one were to understand the creation of a political community.

Now there is is no evidence that clans are essential building blocks for the construction of organized communities and that communities must have clans before they in turn can develop governmental institutions. The early Germanic people seem to have operated with bilateral kinship networks; the Pomo Indians had small matrilineal descent groups which were not linked together in larger clan associations bearing a common name; the Makah had bilateral descent groups. But where clans do exist, they have important consequences. Morgan saw that if you have exogamous clans, then alliance between clans is inevitable since each has to find its spouses outside its own ranks. These alliances imply some form of agreement on the conditions marriage partners can expect and some method of settling disputes when these arise between members of linked units.

It is possible that the Iroquois also appreciated this fact, for Morgan tells us that they claimed to have originated the idea of a division into clans "as a means of creating new relationships by which to bind the people more firmly together" (*League of the Iroquois,* p. 91). Morgan and the Iroquois may thus join those anthropologists who stress that social order rests upon the recognition of the advantage of alliances rather than upon an affirmation of a solidarity based upon descent and allegiances measured by genealogical distance. They would have been in profound disagreement, however, with a common axiom of the alliance proponents: given the Iroquois situation, they could hardly concede that alliances involved the exchange of women between units composed of men.

Morgan noted another aspect of the Iroquois clan, whose significance he chose to ignore because it conflicted with the theory he was building about bounded political units: Iroquois clans were not localized and their membership spread across what appear to be political boundaries. In *League of the Iroquois* he commented that the clans found among the Iroquois were common to all five nations and this "became the means of effecting the most perfect union of separate nations 'ever devised by the wit of men.' " For, as he said, between those of the same clan name "there existed a tie of brotherhood, which linked the nations together with indissoluble bonds" (*League of the Iroquois,* p. 81). He elaborated on this point in *Ancient Society* pointing out that fellow clansmen, whether they might be Mohawks, Oneidas, Onandagas, Cayugas, or Senecas "were brothers and sisters to each other in virtue of their descent from the same common ancestor, and they recognized each other as such with the fullest cordiality." Their first query was about clan membership and then the immediate pedigree of their respective sachems, or council representatives, "after which they were usually able to find, under their peculiar system of consanguinity, the relationship in which they stood to one another" (*Ancient Society,* pp. 185–86).

The discriminating reader will recognize the seeds for a theory of the importance of cross-cutting ties in the maintenance of order and the creation of social cohesion. Max Gluckman and his fellow workers at the Rhodes-Livingstone Institute and the University of Manchester have done much to illuminate the way in which conflict is damped down when people are aligned according to different principles and those to be supported by one principle are those to be opposed according to another. It is possible that the Iroquois were attempting to operate on some policy of creating cross-cutting ties, for Morgan reports that they claimed to have forced a clan system upon the Cherokees, the Chippewas and various others (*League of the Iroquois,* p. 91). But Morgan was trying to build a model of a segmentary system, in which like units combined into a series of yet higher units in what Durkheim later called "mechanical solidarity." Like some anthropologists of the 1940s and 1950s who became fascinated with the complexities of the segmentary lineage model, he largely ignored the implications of the dispersal of clansmen while he dealt with the intermeshing of corporate groups. He worked with the corporate group model rather than the network model.

As a result, he never asked himself certain kinds of questions that would occur to us today as vital for an understanding of what was happening in the region of the Iroquois were attempting to dominate by trade agreements, political pacts, and warfare. In *Ancient Society* (pp. 155–90), Morgan is concerned to demonstrate the existence of the clan principle in other American Indian societies and so provides lists of clans with their associated animal totems. The lists indicate that it ought to have been possible for the Iroquois and their neighbors, whether Algonkian or Iroquoian in speech, to equate their clans and find a basis in clanship to create links comparable to those which he saw as interweaving the Iroquois Confederacy.

Yet he does not examine how the Iroquois handled the uncomfortable fact that they frequently warred upon those whom it may well be they should have treated as kinsmen because of common clanship. Was this what lay behind the practice of adopting foreign captives who were later to be killed by torture —the adoption wiping out any affiliation with Iroquois clansmen who under the rules of clanship would have an obligation to take vengeance? Did they ignore clanship beyond the boundaries of the confederacy and treat all captives as indiscriminate "others?" Or did they invoke clanship when it seemed expedient to do so in order to find terms for dealing with strangers who may have sought to join them or whom they visited on embassy?

Many of us today would regard clanship as a strategy. Morgan, however, was trying to demonstrate that certain kinds of social groupings are appropriate to particular stages of material development. He treated his clans as absolutes, as closed corporations, as units with rigid boundaries, held together by the force of loyalty engendered by ties of descent. In his model of a clan society, therefore, he introduced restrictions that allowed him to say that a great many courses of action were ruled out by definition.

Morgan may have been right about the Iroquois. I am not an Iroquois specialist and do not control enough of the ethnographic and historical data to be able to say whether he is wrong. But the model he built has only a limited utility for understanding how societies with clans use the clan system as a means of promoting order and organizing the population.

My own model is very different: it is derived from trying to understand the clan systems of Central Africa and deals rather with the way the systems are used than with the myth that legitimates them. The clan systems of much of Central Africa have this in common with the Iroquois: they are matrilineal, and clan members are dispersed as residents of different local communities. The Central African clan systems also share with the Iroquois system, and with all clan systems known to me, the crucial feature that clans can be treated as units within the context of the classificatory kinship terminology. That is, if you know a person's clan, you have a good chance of being able to find an appropriate kinship term to signal the etiquette to be used between the two of you and to define the moral imperatives that ought to govern your relationships. Morgan recognized the importance of this last point when he commented that the clan was associated with "a system of consanguinity which reduced all consanguinei to a small number of categories" (*Ancient Society*, pp. 303–304). He concerned himself, however, only with its implications for the internal organization of a clan and did not stress that it had equal significance for the ordering of relationships between members of different clans.

To put it in terms perhaps more comprehensible to an American audience, it works in the same fashion as would the zodiac system if this were integrated with our kinship system. If your father were a Leo, and your mother a Gemini, then all Leos would be your fathers, and all Geminis would be your mothers; while if you were an Aquarius all children of Aquarius would be your children. In a sense, all the world would be kin to you.

In Central Africa, clans have this in common with the signs of the zodiac: they are categories in a system of classification which is inclusive of the human universe. To be recognized as a member of that universe you must be assigned membership in one of the categories of the system. In some parts of the region, the clan system provides the primary sorting which allows people to be placed and so identified and thought about. This was true among the Tonga, who lacked administrative categories, professional categories, class categories, and categories based on either religious associations or age-set associations. Their clan system provided them with an ideal construct or model of the social universe. Their system appears to be rigid in that the number of clans recognized is limited. Again this is an indication of the primacy of the system, since in any classification the primary categories must be few in number if they are to be used effectively in placing smaller units with respect to one another (Simon, 1972: 92).

Tonga do not accept new clans into their system even though their local communities absorb immigrants who come from a distance bringing with them their own clan names and totems. The immigrants are assigned membership in the existing clans by making equations between their totems and those recognized locally; they adopt the local names and are recognized as fellow clansmen, even though people are well aware that they are stretching the fiction of common descent beyond the limits of credibility. Placement in a clan also places the newcomer in relation to members of other clans who regard themselves as sons and daughters, grandchildren, or spouses of the clan. Most of the Tonga of southern Zambia operate with a system of twelve clans. When they brought me within the system by assigning me a clan and a father's clan, at least half the Tonga population, now numbering something like 300,000, could deal with me in kinship terms. Because it is possible to equate Tonga clans with those found outside Tonga country, it would also be possible for me to find my place over much of Zambia, Malawi, Zaire, Angola, and possibly Mozambique.

Among the Tonga, as elsewhere, known kinsmen, of course, are handled as kinsmen and not in terms of clan membership. The two systems are distinct, but they can be intercalated, and so it is possible to move from the clan system into the kinship system, although not, apparently, vice versa. It is also worth emphasizing that Tonga clans did not form corporate groups, choose representatives, or have official leaders who could control the definition of who might be a clan member. The categories were rigidly defined; the application of the categories was left flexible.

Elsewhere in Central Africa, the primary categories were provided either by the units of a centralized state or by an age-set system, and the clan system no longer performed this fundamental task. The number of clans was no longer fixed. Immigrants appear to introduce new clans; these can be accepted into the system without creating major problems either for the immigrants or the prior inhabitants, since newcomers link themselves into the existing structure through clientship, or attachment to an office, or membership in an age-set. Political and ritual offices were distributed among the various clans represented in the system, as among the Bemba, but access to these offices was vested in small lineages whose members monopolized the right to fill them.

It may still be asked why strangers entering the system retain their own clans rather than associate themselves with an existing clan that is linked to an office. Not enough work has been done on the problem. We may find that practice varied with the ruler's ability to create new offices and new political units, thus recognizing the appearance of new constituencies and claimants for position within the power structure. An ambitious newcomer might be able to rise more rapidly in the system by maintaining his distinct identity around which followers could rally. If so, clanship is still a way of organizing a following, but as we would expect, the trade-offs would be different between hierarchical and egalitarian systems.

Morgan dismissed such possibilities by his insistence that clanship was by nature egalitarian and antithetical to hierarchy.

It did not occur to him that it was odd that the Iroquois had so few clans and that the number of clans appeared to be fixed, as in the highly egalitarian Central African model. To be a mem- of the Iroquois universe, one had to be a member of one of these clans, either by birth or adoption. Entry by adoption, however, was rigidly controlled. The Iroquois therefore appear to have held to some principle with respect to optimal population size: the decision to adopt was vested in senior persons, adoption involved a formal ceremony, the person adopted was welcomed into a rigidly defined position within Iroquois society. All these practices were boundary maintaining devices. They prevented the expansion of Iroquois clans to incorporate all those who might have been attracted to join the Iroquois nation.

Morgan argued that they could not expand because they were descent groups, and so limited by the principle which gave them legitimacy. We have seen that this did not apply among the Tonga. It did not apply elsewhere in Africa (Southwold, 1971: 38). For that matter, Iroquois clans were social rather than biological groupings. Morgan himself reported that on one occasion the Hawk clan of the Seneca had been saved from extinction by the adoption of a number of Wolf clansmen who agreed to change their clan (*Ancient Society*, p. 80). Anthony Wallace estimates that some two-thirds of the Oneidas may have been adopted from outside the Confederacy during the periods of most strenuous warfare in the seventeenth century, and he believes that the other Iroquois nations were almost as heavily dependent upon adoption (Wallace, 1970: 103). The decision not to expand must therefore have rested upon some factor other than the belief in common descent.

Again I do not control the Iroquois material sufficiently well to be able to produce the answer, but it does occur to me that their representative system may have been crucial for determining how they viewed the question of clanship. The Iroquois believed the Council of the League had changed little or not at all since its original foundation. It refused to increase its membership to provide representation either for subdivisions of the existing clans or for populations which sought to join it. Even the Tuscarora were refused representation on the Council itself. Under pressure, the Iroquois agreed to create a category of prominent men, but only full council members had the right to vote or the right to present themselves as embodiments of the power of council. None of this is surprising to anyone who has watched the fierce determination with which legislators fight against reapportionment or reforms that might diminish their prerogatives. Given the formal requirement for unanimity, it would be foolish to expect the Iroquois legislature to reform itself. If the clans were conceptualized by the Iroquois as constituencies tied to legislative seats, the constituencies were also frozen.

As some of you may have noted, I have here stood Morgan's argument on its head. Where he argued that the Iroquois government was what it was because it was based on a clan system, I have argued that the Iroquois clan system may have taken the form it did because the Iroquois had vested in its central governing body the right to make certain kinds of decisions and the members of that body had both an interest in resisting actions detrimental to themselves and the ability to do so. I have viewed clanship not as an entity in itself but as a principle of organization which is utilized in different fashions according to the nature of the other institutions existing within the social field. What a clan is, then, is a policy decision. Under some circumstances clans become corporate groups making alliances with one another; under other circumstances, they are categories used as recruiting devices. The interesting question becomes then, not how rules or structures limit action, but *why* people use rules to limit themselves.

In building a model of a society, I suppose today one would ask what are the systems of categorization which allow people to designate and so identify one another and therefore create a framework for interaction. The intellectual tools provided, it then is of some purpose to ask what it is that the members of a society want to organize to achieve—for this defines what exactly they think society is about, as well as what are the evils they see in their present situation. We can begin to understand then the meaning of the limits they set upon themselves.

three

A SOCIETY OF EQUALS: THE PROBLEM OF CONSENSUS

In the last chapter, I dealt with Morgan's assumptions about the nature of government and Morgan's place in the development of anthropological studies of systems of social control. In this chapter I propose to examine the constraints faced by those who live in societies without executive offices or a centralized authority. I shall also be concerned with the role of consensus in such societies.

Morgan assumed that society, before the appearance of highly organized state structures, was egalitarian in nature. He also, of course, assumed that society was under a rule of law, given his belief that government (in the form of the council) was introduced with the origins of the first corporate groups. Anthropologists agree that all human societies by definition possess order (Mair, 1972: 34) but neither they nor the political scientists have reached a consensus about what it is that maintains that order and prevents constant infractions of the social rules. Some have queried whether law in any real sense is possible in the absence of formal institutions for its promulgation and enforcement. Those who build theories about the nature of stateless societies have also differed profoundly in their view of what life is like under such conditions, a difference which rests upon different assessments of the nature of man.

Some, like Hobbes, have seen it as a naked power struggle, based on self-help and an assessment of relative power positions. Hobbes, of course, argued that in the absence of the state writ large, man was in a state of nature, each man at war with his neighbor, leading an existence in which life was "brutal, nasty, and short" (*Leviathan,* p. 188). Some of our contemporaries have accepted the anarchists' vision of man, uncorrupted by government or authority, leading an idyllic life in harmony with his neighbors, following the bent of his own nature. To them, hierarchy, structured social relationships, differentiated roles, and their associated rules of etiquette are an onslaught upon original innocence, rather than an attempt to control original sin. Rousseau, in his youth, may have shared their point of view; for he certainly did say that "the state of nature, being that in which the care for our own preservation is the least prejudicial to that of others, was consequently the best calculated to promote peace, and the most suitable to mankind" (*A Discourse on the Origin of Inequality,* p. 222). His later contention that men had given up their natural liberty for an alliance with their fellows in a community of law in order to obtain security of life and property appears to indicate that he came to lose something of his belief in the benevolence and charity of a mankind untrammeled by civil government (*The Social Contract,* p. 19). It is this, no doubt, that led the nineteenth-century anarchists to repudiate Rousseau's view of society, as they have repudiated others that accepted the discipline of being subject to the law and to social institutions (Woodcock, 1963: 20).

Strangely enough, the assurance that men are basically benevolent toward their fellows apparently was shared by archconservatives who fought the growth of governmental controls and the vesting of power in the hands of government agencies. Herbert Spencer is a much better spokesman for the young in their strictures against authority and their defense of a stage of primal innocence than is Rousseau. Some of Spencer's argument seems to be drawn from Lewis Henry Morgan's work and especially from *Ancient Society.* Spencer shared Morgan's belief that men once lived at peace with one another in a community based upon discussion and compromise and with no need for a formal legal apparatus or officers to enforce the law. Spencer also agreed with Morgan that executive power vested in a magistrate emerged during periods of warfare and grew by adding to itself the functions of judge and priest, and through encroachment upon the rights of the free community. Spencer's statement is worth quoting:

> Be it or be it not true that Man is shaped in iniquity and conceived in sin, it is unquestionably true that Government is begotten of aggression and by aggression. In small undeveloped societies where for ages complete peace has continued, there exists nothing like what we call Government: no coercive agency, but mere honorary headship, if any headship at all. In these exceptional communities, unaggressive and from special causes unaggressed upon, there is so little deviation from the virtues of truthfulness, honesty, justice, and generosity, that nothing beyond an occasional expression of public opinion by informally-assembled elders is needful. Conversely, we find proofs that, at first recognized but temporarily during leadership in war, the authority of a chief is permanently established by continuity of war; and grows strong where successful war ends in subjection of neighboring tribes. (*The Man Versus the State,* p. 112)

Spencer may have sat in his study and cogitated upon the nature of man and society, but some anthropologists who have gone out into the world and met a variety of men living under a variety of forms of government have also been willing to argue that formal controls are largely excess baggage and that men left to themselves still manage to agree and get on with the job of living although they cannot have lives dependent upon an intricate intermeshing of technical processes carried out by diverse persons. Hocart writing in the late 1930s was one who argued that government finally arose, not because men wished to protect themselves or their property from their fellow men, but because they were creating elaborate rituals to make life more bountiful. Elaborate rituals required that different parts of the ceremony be assigned to different actors and that there be a coordinating organization under a master of ceremonies with his subordinates (Hocart, 1970: 34). Again, I think Hocart's view of society is worth quoting:

> We are so used to being governed that we think it the most natural thing in the world, something self-evident. Yet, from Hobbes on, Moderns have always felt that some explanation was needed, that man was not created governed, and that he must at some time have acquired government. So philosophers sat down in a brown study to imagine how it came to pass. They evolved history out of their own consciousness; they wondered how they themselves could get on without government, decided that they could not, that cessation of government would mean anarchy, therefore, they concluded man invented government to get out of anarchy . . . We cannot get on without a central government, because our society is so vast and complex that some coordinating system is needed, for each one has to cooperate with thousands whom he never sees, or even hears of. There are societies where everyone is related to everyone else: they have no need for a coordinating system. They work by mutual understanding . . . members of a hunting tribe are one family; they are born and bred together: they know one another by heart: they are loth to offend one another, because they cannot get away from one another. Even in agricultural communities the ordinary routine is carried on by mutual consent, not by command . . . As a matter of fact we vastly exaggerate the importance of government in our own society . . . the vast, silent, daily work of men and women . . . is the real life of a nation. That daily routine is self-organized. (Hocart, 1970: 128–29)

Hocart's prime example of self-organization and unwritten law is that peculiarly British institution "the law of the queue" which he says "was not made by king and parliament, but is the outcome of a tacit understanding between total strangers very much imbued with respect for the traditional rights of possession." He maintains that the "spontaneous and incessant goodwill" on which such cooperation depends is not "created by government, but on the contrary makes government possible. Without it government would collapse. The most government can do is to remove grit from the machinery." (Hocart, 1970: 129).

Here, as many another has done, Hocart is saying that ultimately government depends upon consensus. He assumes, however, that the basic consensus is an agreement that the rights of others must be respected.

Constraint and Reciprocity

The last several decades have seen a renewed interest in constructing models of the evolution of man and human society. With this there has come an upthrust of the old arguments about the original nature of man, as well as renewed attempts to probe the innate characteristics of his present descendants. I do not propose to enter this discussion. As far as I know there is no way to settle the argument. The fossil record tells us nothing about whether early men loved or despised their fellows. Men were very far from their origins before we have any account of their behavior or of how they treated their fellows on a day-to-day basis. Nor would I assume that the social psychologists' findings on their American victims need tell us much about mankind at large.

There is also a question of how far we are able to understand men and women who stem from very different traditions from our own. Francis Hsu has suggested that western anthropologists, especially Americans, are prone to emphasize aggression as a motivating social force because they themselves have grown up in societies that value individualism and the aggressive pursuit of individual ends. Therefore, he argues, western anthropologists may find it difficult to recognize when people do in fact trust and respect each other and so minimize evidence of cooperation and a willingness to subordinate oneself to the interests of a larger group (Hsu, 1973: 15).

The first question to be answered then is what evidence do we have about how people who lack a formal governmental apparatus see the problem of social control. Here we face the difficulty that no anthropologist, for obvious reasons, has ever studied a society that was completely independent of the control of force exercised through specialized offices. The best we have been able to do is 1) to tap the memories of people who believed that they had recently lived in independent communities where they, not the representatives of some external power, were the ultimate arbiters of their conduct, and 2) to supplement this by observation of what people do in circumstances where they still feel themselves free to act either because external authority is far away or is defined as disinterested in what is done in particular situations. On this basis we now have a respectable number of descriptions of societies whose members say it was left to the individual and his associates to defend his rights. The societies described range in size from small bands with populations of a score or more to some of the segmentary polities encompassing almost a million.

An examination of the ethnographic literature on such societies leads even highly competent anthropologists to different conclusions about the factors that control conflict. Fried (1967: 71, 85–86, 101–104) and Moore (1972: 64–66, 78) are two who have recently made such surveys and come to somewhat different assessments. It might be noted that both are Americans

When two competent persons can reach different conclusions, they must be operating in terms of different assumptions, using different procedures, or looking at different data.

In this case their difference may very well arise from what continues to be a recurrent technical problem for the anthropologist: the ease with which folk-belief can be mistaken for a statement of modal behavior. We listen to informants' fears and to their tales of violence—which Fried has suggested may well be exemplary tales to point a moral rather than accounts of actual happenings—and we diagnose a world of warring factions, or feud, of frequent acts of aggression, mitigated perhaps by the ties of kinship and alliances for mutual self-help against those groups defined for the moment as outsiders. We look around us, however, and we find people apparently behaving with kindness, generosity, and forbearance, avoiding disputes and sharing resources, tolerant of each other's foibles. What we may miss is the connection between the two sets of social facts: the beliefs are related to the behavior. Anthropologists have a liking for paradoxes and it should therefore be no surprise to us if some people live in what appears to be a Rousseauian paradise because they take a Hobbesian view of their situation: they walk softly because they believe it necessary not to offend others whom they regard as dangerous.

The Chimbu of Highland New Guinea are not alone among egalitarian peoples in viewing themselves as fighting animals and fighting as the probable outcome of all conflict: where they seem to be exceptional, along with some other New Guinea highlanders, lies in their failure to avoid conflict as an established policy (Brown, 1972: 19, 56). Lawrence, writing on the same general area, comments, ". . . some societies seem to value peace less than others. Thus, Eastern Highlanders accept bloodshed with a measure of indifference, whereas the Garia are always at pains to arrest conflict." (Lawrence, 1973: 22).

Elsewhere, people appear to regard life in a society approaching anarchy as a test of personal restraint, calling for the control of impulse and the natural man to prevent the breakdown of order and the outbreak of open violence or attack by sorcerers. An absence of external controls calls for the development of internal controls and a recognition that one cannot afford to act out spontaneous emotions.

This at least is the conclusion I have drawn after much discussion with Plateau and Valley Tonga of Zambia who consider that they lived in a state approaching what we would call anarchy in the 1880s and 1890s before they became subject to a colonial administration. They speak of one village raiding another for food in times of hunger, of revenge attacks in which some were killed and others taken captive and enslaved, of the dangers of moving outside one's network of social relations, of the risk of enslavement run by those who asked for food or other benefits from strangers on whom they had no claim, of accused witches burned alive in their huts or thrown into the rapid current of the Zambezi. These are stories. I have no way to assess the frequency with which any of these events may have occurred. They regard it as a true picture. It has many parallels with the way New Guinea villagers describe the way they lived in the 1920s and 1930s before the first Australian patrols arrived. Plateau and Gwembe Tonga attribute such actions to the drive of hunger, the desire for wealth, and to envy, sensitivity to insult, hatred of those who have brought injury, and fear. In fact, they say they fought over the same things which the Chimbu of New Guinea said they had fought over: claims to property and people, and retaliation for insult. They do not see themselves as having fought about ideologies, a fact no doubt related to the formal egalitarianism of their societies, nor did they fight about procedures, unless variance in procedure was seen as insult (Brown, 1972: 56).

The Tonga do not believe that people have changed in nature in recent years. If you ask them why they no longer behave in the manner described, they will say, "because of the Administration," referring to the possibility of intervention by officials of the central power, once colonial and now Zambian.

Nevertheless, external authorities are not resident in each neighborhood and they can give no protection against the flare-up of anger or the covert threat of the sorcerer. The Tonga stress the importance of personal restraint in the interests of avoiding any possibility of raising hackles. They attempt to sidestep issues, are reluctant to allow their fellows to drag them into a dispute, and try to vanish from the scene if those in their vicinity seem intent on pursuing a quarrel. Or close supporters, who inevitably will be identified with the combatants, attempt to restrain them, taking from their hands any weapons or tools which can be used for injury, applying gentle pressure, and murmuring soothing words about the advisability of cooling the combat for the moment. They do not want to take sides and be faced with the consequences of a formal breach with those whom they must continue to encounter within a relatively restricted range nor do they want to draw upon themselves the anger of a vengeful person.

Their tactics do not always work, but by and large they do appear to be successful in damping down outbreaks of open violence an din preventing violence, when it does break out, from spreading beyond the immediate combatants. At times, however, they are on exceedingly thin ice, as they are well aware. The ice is thin because some clash has occurred in the past between every two lineages, every two families, and possibly every two adults on the local scene, and so each and every one has some good reason to hate or fear the rest, kinsmen and nonkinsmen alike.

The ethnographic literature indicates that other people with diffuse and minimal governments—including those who present themselves to the world as truculent warriors and fighters—also live with this fear of violence that brings more violence and that they do their best to restrain behavior that leads to conflict with those regarded as dangerous. Nancy Williams (personal communication) after a review of the literature on Australian Aboriginal conflict found them placing a high premium on the avoidance of actual violence and mobilizing kin to prevent an aggrieved person from going too far. Lenore Ralston (personal communication) from a review of some of the same literature also emphasizes the importance given to devices for limiting the spread of violence. Chowning and Goodenough, writing of the Lakalai, off the coast of New Guinea, report that "parents and elders constantly tell their children and young people what are the likely consequences of improper action. Emphasis is laid on the liabilities to which failure to perform one's duties and to which violating the right of others expose one, and this is consciously exploited as a device for preventing disorder." (Chowning and Goodenough, 1973: 164). Kaberry who worked in New Guinea found Abelam elders actively engaged in trying to damp down the upthrust of hostility:

> If quarreling occurs in their presence, in their own hamlet or elsewhere, they may check it by ridicule or a joke; or, if it is more serious, they counsel moderation, remind the disputants of the misfortunes that have followed from fighting in the past, and assert the importance of ties of kinship. If fighting actually occurs, they wrest spears from those involved, and place the yellow *yauwal* leaf (the symbol of peace), in the centre of the piazza. In situations where an outburst of violence seems highly probable, they try to avert it beforehand by placing a *yauwal* leaf in the piazza and exhorting the younger men not to give way to anger. (Kaberry, 1973: 51)

Pomo Indians with whom I worked in California in the 1930s stressed the importance of passivity under provocation (Colson,

1974: 19); the Makah Indians sweetened the task of showing indifference to insult by assurrances that this was behavior appropriate to the man of rank. The Iroquois installed their council representatives with admonitions that they must have skins "seven thumbs thick" to enable them to withstand the hostility they would encounter, to avoid entering into quarrels, and so present themselves as dignified upholders of order. Hennigh reports of the Eskimo around Point Barrow, "Revenge cycles within the community were . . . greatly feared. Several informants remember fellow villagers, hysterical after the death of a loved one, being physically held down by kinsmen who repeated over and over again, 'Don't kill anyone, don't kill anyone; if you kill somebody their relatives will kill us all.' " (Hennigh, 1972: 90).

Like the Tonga, the Chimbu, the Abelam, the Australians, the Pomo, the Makah, and the Iroquois, the Eskimo believe that conflicts are likely to arise from jealousy, envy, and resentments over insults. Fellow Eskimo are said to be wary of the man who stands on his rights or forces a quarrel upon others, because they have no desire to be drawn into disputes. They prefer "a quiet man." They attempt to deal with the determined trouble-maker by withdrawal of support and if necessary by physical expulsion (Hennigh, 1972: 104, 107; see also, Hughes, 1966).

Eskimo society has been reported as a violent one with a minimum of public control. Yet Robert Spencer has now come to the conclusion that "it was not so much perhaps the presence of feuds . . . as it was the fear of feud" that influenced Eskimo behavior and encouraged the suppression of behavior that could lead to violence (Spencer, 1972: 111).

Clyde Kluckhohn had made much the same argument for the Navaho, another people with minimal government: "the actual helplessness of many people in a scattered and inadequately policed society makes the pattern of playing down aggression on the part of most people a highly adaptive response." He held that in such a society, relatives and associates would punish those who might give way to violence and bring down upon them the violence of others. "A society like the Navaho *must* have harsh sanctions against physical aggression." (Kluckhohn, 1944: 53). Indeed, he believed that aggressive behavior among them had probably become more frequent as Indian Service police took over much of the onus for dealing with violence.

Recent general reviews of the reality of feuding undertaken by Hoebel and Moore independently of each other reach the same conclusion. They find scanty ethnographic evidence for actual feuding in societies said to rely upon self-help, but good evidence for a pervasive fear of feud. Both comment that it is this fear which discourages actions that might lead to violence and the initiation of feud. Hoebel concludes, "Talk about the expected requirements of honor to engage in feud is customarily blown up to feed the fear of the effect of feud." (Hoebel, 1971: 15). He adds, "The fear of feud nourishes and sustains legal systems." Even so, when restraints fail, people may be left confronting each other with no graceful way of withdrawal and feel forced to fight.

Moore agrees that real violence is rare, even though violence is much talked about. She concludes, however, that the absence of formal sanctions in such societies is more apparent than real given that their members were aware that they might be expelled, sold into slavery, accused of witchcraft, or subjected to some other definitive measure if they persisted in reckless disregard of the rights of their neighbors (Moore, 1972: 90). She also suggests that in such societies the rule of strict liability for one's actions may well have a logical connection with the theoretical reliance upon self-help: "In a system in which there is a good deal of freedom of action to use force in one's own interest, abuse of that freedom may be somewhat curtailed by the knowledge that everyone must pay for the consequences of his actions and that the plea of accident or good intention will not excuse one." (Moore, 1972: 67).

The political order of the Luri, a segmentary nomadic people in Iran, who again pay lip service to the feud, has recently been studied by Jacob Black who reports that "one of the most commonly heard words on Luri lips is 'fear.' The need to fear is impressed upon children from the moment they can walk . . . For fear no one ever tells the truth to anyone about any matter of importance. For fear of being waylaid, no man of substance will go anywhere without an escort." Yet he also believes that "it is fear of force rather than force itself" that controls the situation (Black, 1972: 624, 625).

There *is* "peace in the feud" as Gluckman has said (1955: 1–26), but it is a peace based on the prevention of the first act rather than the force which leads to the final settlement.

Against this view, that quarrels are few because people know they must restrain themselves, it has been argued that quarrels may be few because people have little to quarrel about when they have few possessions, lead much the same kind of life, and are on much the same level. Fried is one who argues that among people living in small bands, disputes are rare because few alternative choices are available and people have little incentive to violate accepted standards. He quotes Lorna Marshall as reporting only four observed incidents of interpersonal conflict among members of a Bushman band during the seventeen months she camped near it; during the same period, she heard of, but did not see, three other incidents in neighboring bands (Fried, 1967: 71). From this I agree that it might be possible to conclude that these particular Bushmen avoid overt confrontation. Yet there is evidence that if so, they do so because they are afraid of the consequences rather than because they lack reason for conflict. Elizabeth Marshall Thomas, who lived near the same band, reports that Bushmen have an intense fear of violence. She describes vividly the envy Bushmen feel when one of their number receives a choice item and the use of covert innuendos and implicit threat to force the harrassed individualist to share (Thomas, 1959: 22, 67, 117, 118, 241–42).

Fried appears to minimize both the kinds of conflicts that can arise and the restraints people place upon their behavior. It is all too easy for the short-term visitor to do so in any community. I once took for granted the surface amiability of present Tonga community life but seventeen years of following the members of certain Gwembe Tonga villages have given me a better grasp of their involvement with each other. I now look around a neighborhood gathering and wonder at the tough-minded determination that keeps hostilities from surfacing and disturbing the business of living. Brown makes the same point for the New Guinea Chimbu when she says, "In any small community, over time, there are many grudges and grievances which may be suddenly brought into the open by an immediate conflict. Whenever I attempted to trace back the source of a quarrel, I found that there were many precipitating incidents of disagreement between the parties or the groups in the quarrel." (Brown, 1972: 102).

It is almost certainly false to assume, as Lewis Henry Morgan appeared to do and as Fried apparently does, that people who have few possessions are inclined to place little value on what they have or that they give willingly simply because they give graciously. My own reading of ethnography, and my own experience in a number of American Indian and African societies whose members would be regarded as having had little in the way of material wealth, suggests rather that property is valued, that people are very much aware that possessions give rise to envy, and that they are fearful of the consequences of envy.

They feel themselves constrained to share or to barter their possessions for what they regard as more essential: amicable relationships which ensure their personal safety. They give because they must, but by giving graciously they hope to obtain some benefit from the act. This seems a better explanation than either benevolence or a lack of attachment to possessions for the common practice of pressing an article upon the one who admires it. On the Makah Reservation in the early 1940s, I heard women complain that they had been forced to part with prized possessions because someone had pressured them with admiring comments. They did not want to give, but they gave because they felt they must. Clyde Kluckhohn reported the Navajo as fearing to refuse requests lest the petitioner be a witch (Kluckhohn, 1944: 31–32). Under these conditions, the open coveting of an item can only be some kind of threat, and compliance is an attempt to avoid conflict.

Fear, to most of us, seems a poor basis on which to found a society or develop a system of law. But we are unrealistic if we ignore the fear and concentrate solely on the advantages people see in their associations. A dynamic picture must include them both.

Since the time of Malinowski and Mauss, it has been common to describe human societies as governed by the principle of reciprocity: i.e., it is said their members behave well because they see the advantages to be gained through cooperation with their fellows and recognize that they can extract their due only if they fulfill their obligations. Sahlins recently has written a paean of praise to reciprocity as the organizing force in societies where there is "an absence of a public and sovereign power: persons and (especially groups) confront each other not merely as distinct interests but with the possible inclination and certain right to physically prosecute these interests. Force is decentralized, legitimately held in severalty, the social compact has yet to be drawn, the state nonexistent. So peacemaking is not a sporadic intersocietal event, it is a continuous process within society itself." (Sahlins, 1965: 140). It is by means of exchange, he says, that people in such societies "transcend Hobbesian chaos." And further, exchange "has as its decisive function this . . . instrumental one: the material flow underwrites or initiates social relations" (Sahlins, 1965: 140).

George P. Murdock, one of the most senior of American anthropologists, has recently repudiated much of anthropological theory on the grounds that it deals only with epiphenomena, such as culture and society, but he continues to regard the theory of reciprocity as a major contribution to a science of human behavior. For him, as for Sahlins, reciprocity seems to be an ingredient in personal motivation, rather than a statement about the balance in the system, for he paraphrases Malinowski to produce the following proposition: "the persistence of an element of behavior in an interpersonal relationship depends upon the reciprocally rewarding character of the activities of the interacting individuals" (Murdock, 1971: 22).

This seems to bring us back directly to utilitarianism and the assumption that if each person acts for his own best interests, assuming that he knows them, this results in the greatest happiness of the greatest numbers. This optimistic view is apparently not one shared by people living in societies said to be governed by reciprocity, who may well think of themselves as operating as much in terms of a fear of penalties as in expectation of rewards. Reciprocity works well enough as a concept if our attention is concentrated on a flow of exchanges or on exchanges within dyadic relationships. It is much less satisfactory if we attempt to use it as a general theory of social control, unless we also recognize that it depends on a fear of penalties as well as a hope of reward. This was certainly the way in which Malinowski sometimes used the term to cover the expectations that underwrote the maintenance of order and the flow of social life in Trobriand society (Malinowski, 1926).

Let me cite a recent experience among the Gwembe Tonga. In October, 1972, a visitor entered the homestead of an elderly couple and approached the wife with a request for various kinds of grain to be used for food and planting seed. The two women belonged to the same clan and knew each other slightly, but they lived sufficiently far apart so that they rarely met, except when the visitor passed through the village of her host on her way to the nearby dispensary. After chatting, the housewife went to her granary and drew out enough grain to fill the visitor's basket to overflowing, meanwhile continuing her conversation with her visitor. The latter was sharing a meal with other women in the homestead. The treatment of the visitor was in the best traditions of Tonga hospitality and the gift of grain was made with every indication of gracious generosity. These are the data.

There are various ways of interpreting the incident. With Morgan, we could attribute the housewife's response to the overriding imperatives of the kinship bond which makes it natural for kinsmen to help each other. The woman who asked for grain would say the bond of clanship legitimized her request and that it is right that clansmen help each other. The housewife may have been encouraged to be generous because she was aware that she too may need assistance in the future and wished to maintain ties with kinsmen in other localities which would give her the right to draw on their supplies or assistance in an emergency. Again the woman who asked for grain would no doubt say, if asked, that she in turn would expect to help a fellow clanswoman in need. The stress on clanship would, of course, allow the credits and debits within the system to be balanced out among all members of the clan rather than between the two individuals. We therefore can use this as in instance supporting the theory of reciprocity. The two explanations are mutually reinforcing, although one emphasizes that it is morally right to support one's kin while the other would emphasize that it is economically advantageous to do so.

The housewife made no comment on her action at the time and I am afraid I interpreted it as a gift to secure the future and to reinforce kinship links regarded as long-term social insurance. I based my interpretation partly on a knowledge of the uncertainty of local harvests and the frequency with which people have had to appeal to kinsmen in other areas when crops have failed, even in these days when they can also expect some assistance from government. I also, of course, was inspired by anthropological theory and delighted to recognize one transaction in a system of generalized reciprocal exchange (Sahlins, 1965: 147). The housewife disillusioned me some weeks later, while lecturing a young man temporarily resident in the village on the wisdom of giving food to those who asked for it.

The young man had just received a disturbing letter from home: one evening, lights had been seen about his granary and his wives and brother had later found evidence that ghosts had urinated over the grain, an act which Tonga believe ghosts carry out only if sent by a sorcerer. He told us about the matter, speculating about who had wanted to kill him and his family and what he should do to save the grain and protect them all in the future. He was very bitter, saying that his ambition of the previous year—which had led him to work early and late in the large field he had planted—was now bringing him only a harvest of hate. He was inclined to blame neighbors who had not worked as hard and now envied him the reward of his labor.

The housewife commented that there must be those who envied him his good fortune when they saw his large granaries, either because they had little food themselves or because they were angry because he had so much. She thought someone must have visited his homestead and seen all the granaries, and she asked if he could remember anyone having stood to gaze at them or asking for food or making any comment about all that food. She pointed out that he could not know what kinds of medicine a person might have or who might be a sorcerer. "It is not safe to deny them. You saw me give grain to that woman who came the other day. How could I refuse when she asked me for grain? Perhaps she would do nothing, but I could not tell. The only thing to do is to give."

As the people within the homestead discussed the two incidents, it became obvious that each one accepted the premise that given the impossibility of knowing whether someone had the power to injure you, each request should be treated as though it came from someone who might be dangerous. It seemed perfectly reasonable to them that one should give to avoid possible retaliation.

In their discussion, they were guided by a common Tonga belief that the sight or smell of good food that one is not allowed to share causes people to feel envy and hatred towards the fortunate possessors and that the envious who are associated with ghosts send these to poison the coveted food, so that those eating, and their descendants, may ever after be allergic to that particular kind of food. A great many Tonga have food taboos said to have originated when they or their ancestors ate of an abundant supply of food which had aroused the envy of someone in the community. Frequently the alleged sorcerer is said to have been a kinsman or a near neighbor. Tonga also say that if one has a good thing one does not wish to share, then it should be hidden and eaten in secret—refusal to share is both discourteous and dangerous.

In 1957 I saw and heard a dramatic demonstration of their belief that disputed food is dangerous. A hippo had been killed by a government game guard to provide meat for the people of one neighborhood. Although the Gwembe Tonga keep livestock and are better off for protein than many African people, meat is scarce and Tonga speak often of meat hunger, for which they have a special term. The government employees decided to simplify the distribution process by dividing the meat into four equal piles—one for their own headquarters and one for each of the three villages in the neighborhood, although this was patently inequitable since the sizes of the villages ranged from 45 to 300. The employees then departed and the fight began, as each one present tried to seize what meat he could. The headman of the largest village lost the portion designated for himself in the midst of the melée. When he traced the meat, he summoned a meeting and the case was heard. Those in possession of the meat denied having stolen it, but said they gladly gave it to the headman as he had claimed it. He refused to take it. They refused to take it back. No one would take it. Eventually it was thrown away. People explained to me that, after all the quarreling, they were afraid to use meat that must by now have attracted the attention of the ghosts.

I would not suggest for a moment that the Tonga or any other people do not engage in direct exchange or enter into contracts with each other from which they expect to obtain mutual advantage. But exchanges and contracts are likely to be either highly specific, with an understanding of just what it is each party is expected to do, or they involve people who are in constant contact so that giving and return can be balanced at short intervals and the advantages to each partner easily assessed. Their problem, and that of many other people in small face-to-face communities, lies in the fact that they cannot easily terminate a relationship if the return is unsatisfactory, either because other may insist that the relationship still exists or because they are afraid to anger someone they suspect of having greater power. Ultimately they are forced to find allies who will agree that withdrawal is legitimate and will assist them in facing down their opponents. What appears to keep the situation under some kind of control is a mutual fear, the awareness that each party is vulnerable if there are not checks on the sorcerer or the man of violence, and the acknowledgement that there are circumstances in which it is possible to repudiate kin or other associates.

If appreciation of the advantages of cooperation and equitable exchange were the sole controlling element in social life among people such as the Tonga, we could dispense with any concept of community or society as an entity greater than the sum of its parts as Murdock has suggested we ought to do and as some of our colleagues have already done. A collection of individualists freely negotiating with each other and regarding all aspects of their relationship as open to negotiation does not make a moral community or require law. This is a point made by Gluckman in his recent comment that many of the younger social anthropologists "have moved from the emphasis laid by their elders on social relationships to study human action apart from the constraining effect of custom" (Gluckman, 1972*b*: 2). For his word "custom," I would substitute "public opinion" or "the public interest," both of which imply standards against which the action is assessed by bystanders who may have no immediate interest in the advantage gained by any of the contenders or actors but who do have a concern for the possible impact upon the general tenor of their own lives and so provide an ultimate court of appeal. They are the ones who apply what Bailey has called the "normative rules" (Bailey, 1969: 4–5) and so judge contestants as well as contest.

Standards and Consensus

Whether we call them customs, laws, usages, or "normative rules" seems of little importance. What is important is that communities such as the Tonga do not leave their members free to go their own way and explore every possible avenue of behavior. They operate with a set of rules or standards which define approprite action under a variety of circumstances. The rules, by and large, operate to eliminate conflict of interests by defining what it is people can expect from certain of their fellows. This has the healthy effect of limiting demands and allowing the public to judge performance. It is old knowledge in anthropology that rules have the effect of channeling hostilities by defining who it is who may be in competition for certain kinds of benefits.

Gluckman and some of his colleagues have done much to focus the attention of anthropologists on the existance of conflict within society. They see it as produced by rules which give various contenders legitimate but divergent claims to the same resources or else that the rules create moral dilemmas because people are expected to be guided by values that require opposing courses of action (Gluckman, 1965; Middleton, 1966; Turner, 1957, 1966). They find in ritual an attempt to transcend particular interests and contending claims by an appeal to more universal themes about which there can be no dispute.

At another level, however, they would see conflict as endemic to social life because people who live in close juxtaposition use the same space and want support and attention from the same individuals. Rules, even though they may at times produce conflict, reduce the chances for conflict because they reduce the total amount of ambiguity for those concerned by defining specific rather than universalistic claims and obligations. It becomes possible to order one's life with a set of priorities regarded as legitimate. The merit of any particular action can be argued, or whether or not some other priority should have been chosen on this occasion, but the recognition of the right to allocate is an important defense for the individual. Any anthropologist who has had a long extended period of field work in a very different society will understand precisely what I am saying; for the fact that we have no obvious obligation to give to one rather than to another or to channel our friendships and support makes us fair game to all. The priorities we set up for ourselves are neither self-evident nor necessarily acceptable when they are known, and we arouse expectations we cannot fulfill. Among the Tonga I have had to learn that I should not give just because I feel like giving as this is an insult to all who do not receive. Rules do not solve all problems; they only simplify life.

They also give a framework for organizing activities. Standards and some means of applying sanctions are necessary complements to the rules if a system of social control is to operate within a community. Among people such as the Tonga, onlookers apply the standards of performance in particular roles in making an overall judgement about the total person; this in turn allows them to predict future behavior. Judgment is an ongoing process through which consensus is finally reached.

The ultimate sanctions, which once included exile, ostracism, or death, were invoked apparently only to abort what "the criminal" *might* do and never in punishment for what he *had done*. For what he had done was only an offense against individuals and therefore of no public concern, unless he had misguidedly attacked religious symbols associated with the general interest. Radcliffe-Brown pointed out long ago that the one public crime in such societies was often that of being a bad character. This is consistent with the nature of such communities, for any other offense could only affect particular interests and give rise to private claims. The decision that someone is "a bad character" cannot be reached on the basis of any one adjudication—it is a consensus achieved only after discussion and the pooling of a variety of experiences, all carrying much the same implication.

Only an individual, and his supporters, are interested in what a man has done, for this is the basis of their claim for compensation. The general public, on the other hand, is interested in what he is and can be expected to do in the future since this is a guide to the risks they encounter in dealing with him. It gives them some incentive to assess what has happened on particular occasions, but little reason to ensure that compensation in fact be paid or punishment administered. This forward-looking character of the system of social control operating among people like the Tonga is one of the reasons why their legal systems appear to be so different from our own formal legal system, though they are like enough to the informal systems of control that still operate in closeknit local communities in Europe and America since there too it is possible to reach a general consensus about people rather than about crimes (see Gluckman, 1965: 206, 263–64).

The creation of such a consensus is a gradual process and is dependent on the existence of a dense social network since it requires frequent meetings among those who are involved with the same people. Members of the community are thereby able to pool information, assess both the indications of approval or disapproval, and the credibility attached to various allegations. Standards for appropriate behavior are adduced and those who are the focus of the conversation are measured against the standards. Walter Sangree, who described the Tiriki elders of western Kenya wandering from beer drink to beer drink, encountering each other daily at informal gatherings called for other purposes, has shown us the setting for the creation of their common consensus and the judgement of the public (Sangree, 1966: xxxvii, 282–83). A formal hearing drew on this background, "once a case is presented, the whole life and character of the accuser and the accused are potentially on trial, and to a lesser extent this is also true of the witnesses" (Sangree, 1966: 90).

Emrys Peters, in a stimulating recent article on social control in the Welsh countryside, has outlined the whole process whereby public opinion becomes mobilized through gossip at work parties and among groups of young men who meet nightly and pool their knowledge of what their elders feel about this one and that. Recent events are assessed and against this an assessment of character established. Ultimately the youths, who are somewhat marginal to the society, take action against those who are deemed to have violated the local standards, by the playing of tricks, which their elders officially deplore but also tolerate (Peters, 1972).

In eighteenth-century Iroquois society, according to Wallace:

> Behavior was governed not by published laws enforced by police, courts, and jails, but by oral tradition supported by a sense of duty, a fear of gossip, and a dread of retaliatory witchcraft. Theft, vandalism, armed robbery, were almost unknown. Public opinion, gently exercised, was sufficient to deter most persons from property crimes, for public opinion went straight to the heart of the matter: the *weakness* of the criminal. A young warrior steals someone else's cow—probably captured during a raid on a white settlement—and slaughters it to feed his hungry family. He does this at a time when other men are out fighting. No prosecution follows, no investigation, no sentence; the unhappy man is nonetheless severely punished, for the nickname 'Cow-killer' is pinned to him, and he must drag it rattling behind him wherever he goes. People call him a coward behind his back and snicker when they tell white men, in his presence, a story of an unnamed Indian who killed cows when he should have been killing men. (Wallace, 1970: 25–26)

If people meet rarely and their circles of acquaintances do not overlap extensively, they have little possibility of developing common norms or of reaching a consensus about each other (Bott, 1971: 60); they must continue to respond to individual acts or depend upon impersonal laws. When the Tonga woman begged for grain, she aroused the suspicions of the woman she approached, but since the two women lived in different neighborhoods, that suspicion could not be pooled with other information to establish her reputation as a sorcerer. If she begged constantly within her own neighborhood or immediate vicinity or from various members of some one other community, the information would be pooled and the consensus established. Tonga not only recognize sorcery as a possible skill, they identify and fear the sorcerers in their midst. Eventually they may proclaim them through recourse to a diviner, usually one from outside the local community, who can and does focus public opinion without provoking charges of bias (Colson, 1966).

Before this stage is reached, people may have recourse to other institutionalized means of warning an offender that he or she is antagonizing public opinion. Song makers who have the aegis of the ancestral shades for their practice may dwell upon heinous misdeeds and the young people dance to songs which carry their message of ridicule and condemnation. Joking partners of various kinds, who have a general obligation to trade insults, sharpen their insults with reference to condemned behavior.

These are common devices used also by other people who depend upon diffuse sanctions, either because they have no institutionalized formal authorities to invoke or because they prefer to deal with particular situations through informal means. Among the Tonga, however, the knowledge that people are gossiping carries the threat that the ancestral shades will become angry and intervene in association with malevolent ghosts. In the past the build-up of gossip and reproach would have signaled to the individual involved a need for reform or for a quick move to another region. He would have become aware that by this stage, direct action against him would probably be safe, because his kinsmen and associates would have been apprised that they would have no general backing if they attempted to defend or revenge the condemned if anyone wished to proceed against him.

Where people are not in frequent contact, and a dense social network does not exist, they may have a category which would imply condemnation but be unable to designate members of that category. Paul Baxter (1972) has described the general absence of witchcraft and sorcery accusations among East African pastoralists. They believe in witches and sorcerers, as do their agriculturalist neighbors, but rarely make direct accusations against specific persons. Pastoralists move frequently for good ecological reasons without expectation that the people who are together one season ever will reassemble either at the same or some other pasture. Baxter points out that their lives encourage separation and herders remain together only if they like one another sufficiently to make a determined effort to cooperate. Since the normal incidents of life give adequate excuse for people to move apart, they do not need the explosive force of a witchcraft accusation to legitimize their separation from others (Baxter, 1972: 179). He believes this may be the explanation for the absence of accusations. I suggest that even more to the point is the fact that what a man does on one occasion does not become added to a community dossier—each person moves on to associate for a period with those who have no reason to be interested in his former companions. They therefore have no way to pool information and so provide for suspicions to be clarified and consensus reached.

If I am right, this might explain an observation Clyde Kluckhohn once made to me. At the time he wrote *Navaho Witchcraft* in the early 1940s, he had been able to record many statements about the nature of witchcraft and much evidence that Navajos feared witches, but he knew of few instances where actual illness had been attributed to specific witches (only eight cases in more than 1,000) or of instances where specific persons had been accused as witches (Kluckhohn, 1944: 31). In the next decade or so, he heard much of current accusations and suspicions against specific neighbors and kin. He told me he did not know whether Navajo told him more as his knowledge of their life and their language increased or if a real change in frequency of accusation had occurred. If the Navajo in fact were able to meet more often during the later years and if their social networks were becoming denser, then one would expect them to be more frequently in situations where they were able to create the kind of consensus about individuals which permitted them to proclaim rather than suspect the witch.

This explanation would be in line with Kluckhohn's observation that among the scattered Navajo population "intensified gossip is not as satisfying an outlet as it seems to be in a society like Zuni" whose people lived close together in a village "where everyone knows everyone else" (Kluckhohn, 1944: 53, 55). The Zuni, like other Pueblo Indians of the Southwest, are noted for their fear of witches and the frequency with which those who step out of line are accused as witches (Parsons, 1927).

In societies such as these, insofar as communities have a continuity in personnel, social life means the submission of the individual to the constant judgement of peers. Friedenberg, in *The Anti-American Generation,* has characterized the older generation of Americans as taking the moral view

> that it is wrong to antagonize people if you can avoid it, or to be arrogant or uncompromising or to make a divisive display of one's personal views or idiosyncracies, or to spoil a good team play by acting out on your own. The rationale for this moral position is, of course, derived from the demands of consensus politics in the small group as well as the state. To behave in such a fashion as to destroy consensus or even impede its formation is immoral because it is held to be impractical and counter-productive. It disrupts negotiations, and may lose you and your associates their turn next time and their share in the negotiated settlement. (Friedenberg, 1971: 6)

If one substituted "dangerous" for "impractical and counter-productive," one would be close to the point of view of the Tonga and members of other societies organized on egalitarian principles or even in small chieftaincies where safety was seen to depend upon alliances with neighbors whom one could not afford to antagonize (see, for example, Wilson, 1971: 86–87). The communities in which all these people lived were governed by a delicate balance of power, always endangered and never to be taken for granted: each person was constantly involved in securing his own position in situations where he had to show his good intentions. Usages and customs appear to be flexible and fluid given that judgement on whether or not someone has done rightly varies from case to case, as Heesterman among others has pointed out (1973: 97). But this is because it is the individual who is being judged and not the crime. Under these conditions a flouting of generally accepted standards is tantamount to a claim to illegitimate power and becomes part of the evidence against one.

four

THE LIMITS OF AUTHORITY: KNOWING THE RULES

The general theme of this book is the problem of social order and the implications of public controls. In the previous chapter, I have discussed the nature of social control in egalitarian societies, those defined by Mair as having minimal or diffuse governmental institutions, and have attempted to demonstrate that this control rested upon a belief that men must restrain themselves if they are to live together. They do not lack occasion for quarrels and hostility but they learn that they must control their hostility, their greed, and their envy if they are to survive. I also dealt with the process whereby a public consensus was achieved which enabled such communities to place under ban those who consistently went their own way. In this chapter, I propose to examine what happens as members of such societies are drawn into the orbit of a centralized administration having formal institutions for the maintenance of law and order.

Liberty and Authority

Despite our own emphasis upon both freedom of expression and the advantages of egalitarianism, there is no reason to believe that those who live under conditions of "ordered anarchy" believe the two to be associated. Nor indeed do we have reason to believe that they think their situation to be ideal in their freedom from external controls (Wilson and Wilson, 1945: 115). After they become subject to a colonial rule or to the rule of one of the successor states, they may look back and idealize their former freedom from the intervention of police or other officials. Many, however, are prepared to discuss the advantages and disadvantages of the old system with its pressure for conformity and restrictions on mobility. As we have seen, the people felt the constraints of the self-control necessary if they were to avoid bringing their neighbors down them and also felt the strain of being on guard against encroachment. They recognized that they lived in danger that the peace would be broken and the community disrupted. Lewis Henry Morgan's belief that societies change because men seek to better their lot and to find solutions to the evils of their condition may be less foolish than it appeared to be in the days when we believed with Durkheim that men sacralized their societies and revered the conditions in which they found themselves.

I have long since learned, during the three decades in which I have continued to revisit the Tonga of Zambia and followed their development, that when I place high value on certain aspects of Tonga life, I am responding to my own philosophy and appreciation of the problems of my own American society and not necessarily seeing through Tonga eyes. Institutions and principles which I regard as integral to the working of their order, may be regarded by them as necessary evils or be debated as to their relevance or desirability. I suspect much the same is true elsewhere and that this is one of the reasons why anthropologists are now questioned in many parts of the world where we have worked as the people we describe come to read our books and say that we have valued them for the wrong reasons.

The anthropologist may see the significance of the beliefs in sorcery for the maintenance of systems of exchange or of familial and community control, but it is very likely that many people would be prepared to jettison their social systems if thereby they could get rid of the sorcerers and their fear of sorcery. They might even be willing to settle some of their conflicts if they thought that this would allow them to throw out some of their rituals.

Knowing the evils of one's situation and doing something about them are very different matters. Change, as we all know, is difficult: 1) it is not easy to thnk of good solutions to existing problems; 2) the genius who does think of one rarely has the resources to provide experimental evidence that the solution will work; 3) if people have little margin, they are not prepared to adopt radical departures from practices that have worked unless results are certain; 4) they want a guarantee. This last means either an assurance that the new solution will work or an adequate answer to the question, "What will we do if it doesn't work?"

Since major changes produce an increase in ambiguity for the time being, with a consequent loss of predictability, promised rewards must be pretty substantial to offset the fears aroused (Scudder, 1973). Morgan quotes the Iroquois on the difficulties they believed they faced in bringing into existence the confederacy which was to guarantee their internal peace. Wallace, as we have seen in Chapter Two, suggested that the guarantee for the new Iroquois dispensation must have been the assurance that supernatural powers were behind the program, just as the reforms of Handsome Lake at the end of the eighteenth century were underwritten by the message he brought from the world other than this world. Wilson Wallis (1918, 1943) has long since demonstrated how commonly throughout the world the guarantee is associated with a messiah. On occasion, however, the guarantee that makes people willing to experiment appears to be due to the intrusion of representatives of some external power whose support can be invoked to force compliance and so create the order that in turn legitimates itself. The saviors from outer-space, or even the barbarians, are some kind of a solution.

Aidan Southall (1956) has shown how small communities with minimal governments along what came to be the Ugandan–Zaire border attempted to create an overarching order by adopting princes of the Alur ruling house. They hoped through this to be able to negotiate with one another and settle various disputes and so transcend the limitations of their small-scale world. The princes were thought to have power over both men and nature; this made the prince, and not some local leader promoted for the purpose, the appropriate vehicle of the desired order. The princes, and their immediate accompanying entourages, proceeded to enforce the peace they were thought to create.

The ease with which colonial administrations established themselves in some parts of Africa and New Guinea, with a minimal deployment of force, may well be due to a comparable desire for an overriding authority to ensure the public peace and provide a better mechanism for settling disputes than one based on threat and counter-threat. This is what appears to have happened in parts of Highland New Guinea where people such as the Fore are reported to have accepted the advance of representatives of the Australian administration as a solution to the endemic warfare that bedeviled them. Sorrenson reports that they regarded warfare as a curse which they had found no way of abolishing by themselves. He say, "It ceased almost spontaneously with the distant arrival of the first Australians. The warfare was not liked, and the distant presence of but a single patrol officer and a handful of native police was grasped as an excuse to cease" (Sorrenson, 1972: 360). He goes on to describe how most Fore groups did not even wait to be told to stop fighting by the new administration. They

> stopped on their own—almost as if they had only been waiting an excuse to give it up . . . The Fore said among themselves that the . . . government officer . . . was coming so it was time to stop the fighting. They looked to his arrival as the beginning of a new era rather than as an invasion. Disputes which could not be settled by the Fore themselves were eagerly put into the hands of the patrol officers for arbitration, and an antifighting ethic quickly spread throughout the region. (Sorrenson, 1972: 362)

The Chimbu, another belligerent Highland New Guinea population, are reported by Brown as having been somewhat less appreciative of the coming of the new order, but they too "often expressed gratitude for the new peace and security." Chimbu men often found "the new life dull," but even they never suggested that they wanted a return to the old days recalled by them as a time of recurrent raid and counter-raid (Brown, 1972: 57).

Over much of North America, the coming of Europeans had a contrary effect and led to an increase in warfare. Native Americans viewed representatives of the federal government, not as a usable arbitrator in local disputes, but as the immediate ally of white settlers already overrunning their lands. Integration into the larger political unit came with total defeat. Treaties may have stipulated the conditions on which they acquiesced to incorporation, but nothing in the encounter can have endeared the new order to them. In South America at the present time, the same tragic total defeat is being experienced by Native Americans in the Amazon basin as their territories are being preempted for "modern development." Nevertheless, we do have an account of the Yąnomamö who live along the Brazilian–Venezuelan border, written by an anthropologist who worked among them before the governments of the two countries involved had established control or were able to intervene in the local wars (Chagnon, 1968). Hallpike, in a recent article on warfare, writes,

> The Yąnomamö, like . . . other acephalous societies, engage in warfare because among other reasons they cannot stop, not because they necessarily as a culture derive any benefit from fighting. In the absence of any central authority, they are condemned to fight forever, other conditions remaining the same, since for any one group to cease defending itself would be suicidal. In some cases of this type the people have no real desire to continue fighting, and may welcome outside pacification. (Hallpike, 1973: 454)

If by "pacification," he means that they would welcome restrictions on their neighbors that would in turn allow them to relax their own vigilance, then he may well be right.

Certainly elsewhere those who are caught up in the transformations attendant upon the increasing role of the modern state, whether it be colonial or newly independent, may have some nostalgia for the interdependence characteristic of the earlier, self-contained, egalitarian local communities, from which escape was once difficult. But this is offset by their appreciation of the advantages to be found in the new freedoms. Older people at least do not take these for granted, and they see them as dependent upon the maintenance of an overarching central order (Wilson and Wilson, 1945: 115).

In the recent spate of criticism of the obvious burdens and injustices imposed by governments and their chosen agents upon those governed, it is sometimes assumed that the values of egalitarianism and personal freedom are so overriding that governments resting on any but the most diffuse base of discussion must be tyrannies sustained only by force. Black, who has written an account of the political and economic systems of contemporary Luristan, in Iran, where nomads are being made subject to the central government, argues that "men consent to the structures which are forced upon them, and no more" (Black, 1972: 631). It does not appear to have occurred to him that men may see governments as providing services for them, services which they cannot see themselves capable of providing and, if necessary, they are prepared to pay the cost of that service.

We cannot understand the history of the colonial period, or indeed the history of our own time, if we do not undertsand that people may be prepared to accept authority, even though they find it both threatening and frustrating, because they see it as the guarantor of an overarching security which they value or as promising a security that is lacking. Those who challenged the colonial governments in a search for more local control and then for independence were not seeking a return to the precolonial system of diffuse controls (see, for example, Sangree, 1966: 230).

In 1962, when African political leaders within Zambia were trying to mobilize the popular sentiment for the creation of an independent state with an African-dominated government, older Valley Tonga who remembered the precolonial days had one primary apprehension—they did not want to return to conditions they remembered when they had had to depend upon themselves for ensuring life and property, rather than on the presence of the district administration, and the more remote central government. I am not suggesting that they loved either the district administration or the higher echelons of government. They had many complaints against the colonial system and its assault upon their dignity. Several years earlier they had been completely alienated from the central government and its representatives, or so it seemed, because it had taken much of their land to create Lake Kariba one of the largest man-made lakes in the world, and resettled them against their will (Colson, 1971; Scudder, 1962). But when faced with what they thought might be a choice between government and anarchy, they said they wanted government. Their attitude very much resembled that described by newspaper reports on fears common throughout Highland New Guinea in 1972 and 1973 as the people faced the coming of an independent New Guinea.

During the years when political movements were growing throughout Africa, colonial officials and other Europeans shared a common delusion that Africans were contented with their lot unless they were beguiled by "trouble-makers." This was nonsense, of course. African political leaders had no need to teach the people dissatisfaction with their political and economic situation or with a system that gave disproportionate advantages to Europeans. They did have to convince people that they had the ability to take over and administer a state apparatus. It helped, of course, if they could demonstrate that the Europeans could no longer operate the apparatus and so there was less to lose in experimenting with African leadership. In Zambia, with the transfer of power in 1963 and 1964, those Valley Tonga who had been most dubious recognized that government was an entity in itself and not the property of the Europeans: the general framework of order was not going to dissolve around them. With that, they returned to their normal determination that government controls were not to impinge upon the conduct of their lives if they could prevent it, while at the same time they complained that government was remiss in that it was failing to provide them with good roads, marketing facilities, health services, improved schooling and other services they now regarded as among the purposes for which government is instituted.

For a brief period, while the final outcome of the struggle for political control appeared to be in question, villagers held the happy belief that the political opponents who sought to control "government" were so aware of a need for their support that they themselves could define the limits of governmental authority, control the behavior of its officers, and obtain from government the benefits they desired. During this period they actively used the apparatus of the political party and the political campaign, both associated with a legislative assembly, for pressing programs and policies they desired and demanding that the executive live according to the rules. But as leaders of the drive for independence have become entrenched in power and have become government rather than providing an alternative channel of protest, local people once again tend to see government as external to their system.

The Useful Court

The importance given to the control of violence and the finding of more effective means of settling disputes within communities and across community boundaries, which are recurrent problems in egalitarian societies, is to be seen in the general popularity accorded to the introduction of formal court systems with established personnel. These were created by colonial administrations and given a mandate to summon parties in dispute with their witnesses, to hear evidence, and to pronounce a judgment with power of enforcement. Courts might be seen as venal or sometimes as involved in an attack upon persons and property via their messengers and other personnel. They might be condemned as instruments through which unwanted rules introduced from above were inflicted upon a reluctant people. Their general utility, however, was still recognized. This was true in New Guinea (Berndt, 1973: 419; Lawrence, 1973: 29; but also see Hatanaka, 1973). It was true in Africa.

Since the publication of Evans-Pritchard's classic monograph (1940), the Nuer of the Sudan have been the epitome of the egalitarian stateless society whose members defended their rights by resort to self-help and feud. British administration was extended into their country only in the late 1920s and 1930s. By the 1940s, Howell found the Nuer competing for the establishment of new local courts or using the threat of a court suit to force opponents to settle claims (Howell, 1954). The Tiv of Nigeria, another classic egalitarian segmentary polity, proceeded in much the same fashion to adopt the newly instituted courts and use them alongside their own system of moots, using the threat of appeal from moot to court and from lower court to higher court to force litigants to accept decisions (Bohannan, 1957: 14). In the 1950s, the Arusha of Tanzania continued to use methods of social control based on negotiation between lineages and age-sets, while at the same time appreciating the advantages of the local courts established by the administration for handling disputes with strangers or in forcing a settlement (Gulliver, 1963). The Lugbara of Uganda, who had lacked formal institutions of chieftainship and courts, found the new courts the appropriate place in which to settle quarrels between Lugbara sections which once would have given rise to feud (Middleton, 1966: 151). The Tonga of Zambia like the others have been reluctant to accept an adverse court decision, but they are in complete agreement that courts are a highly desirable institution.

In no community do people rely solely upon the existence of courts for adjudicating disputes and maintaining order. Even the once egalitarian peoples who have come to accept a court system as desirable continue to use other methods in most instances. But they recognize that the existence of courts provides them with a possibility of escape from some kinds of dependence upon their fellows. They travel more easily now when they know they have the protection of courts, even in regions where they have neither kinsmen nor other supporters. Although they recognize that court members are likely to favor local people against strangers, they know they are not completely at the mercy of only one court because it is part of a larger system. They can appeal a decision, and the reputation of the court is a matter that concerns its members who can be discharged or penalized for blatant bias. Bias is the easier to perceive because the courts are expected to give judgement based on the merits of each case and not on the merits of those involved in the dispute —a feature distinguishing them from the old methods of social control discussed in Chapter Three.

Men and women also discover a new freedom in their home communities as they are relieved of some of the strain of conformity to local opinion. They no longer have to approach their fellows in the fashion once necessary when they had to obtain supporters who would help them to press or fight a complaint. The Tonga point out that if they have a grievance they now can go directly to the court; they need not spend time convincing kinsmen that the matter is sufficiently important to make it worth running the risks inherent in the confrontation that takes place when two sets of supporters face each other in a local hearing or moot. For that matter, people no longer need to be so concerned to ingratiate themselves with their kin in the hope of future support and they are freer to refuse to give their own support. Each person can live more freely of himself and make his own decisions.

Men and women can also sometimes extract an acknowledgement of their claims simply by threatening to go to court because opponents want to be spared a long walk, the ordeal of questioning, and the possibility of a court fine, as well as an unfavorable decision. Settlement of disputes within a neighborhood is easier than before and less likely to mobilize contending factions. On the other hand, however, it is very likely that claims which previously would have been suppressed to avoid a conflict are now allowed to surface.

The Tonga also appreciate the fact that the courts, because of their association with a police force, have the power to see that judgments are carried out, something the local moot could not do since it had no executive officers. In the latter forum, everyone might agree that a claim was justified, but unless the plaintiff wanted to start a fight by seizing property belonging either to his opponent or an associate of his opponent, he might still have to wait for settlement until a counterclaim arose and gave him bargaining power.

How difficult it was to collect claims under the old system, I became aware from listening to Gwembe village moots where some of the old procedures are still invoked. One case heard in 1963 involved a young man who was being sued for elopement damages. He admitted he ought to pay the damages and he recognized he *must* pay the damages before his sweetheart's guardian would agree to legitimize the marriage by accepting bridewealth. But her father was also insisting that the lover accept responsibility for settling a debt left by his long-dead mother's brother and that this debt must be paid before any agreement would be made on the elopement damages. The elders involved in the hearing, including those supporting the young man, were men who stood in multiple debt relationships to each other; therefore, they could not repudiate the validity of such a claim without endangering their own claims. They could only agree that the debt ought to be paid. This left the young man vulnerable since he was the only one whose immediate interests could force him to settle. The local courts, which are expected to decide each case on its merits rather than as one episode in a total set, would have separated the two cases and concerned themselves only with the elopement damages. On the other hand, the young man could solve his immediate dilemma by running away from the moot, which had no authority given it by the administration to enforce its decision. The local courts, which hold individuals responsible for their own actions, are also able to summon them to return to the court's jurisdiction to pay awarded damages and can further assess fines for contempt of court against those who refuse to pay.

It is a common axiom among anthropologists that local courts and moots in Africa, and often elsewhere, whether newly instituted by colonial administrations or based on long tradition, seek to deal with breaches in relationships among members of an ongoing community and so widen the scope of their investigation beyond that acceptable in an American or European court (Gluckman, 1965: 183–96; Nader, 1969; Van Velsen, 1969: 137–50). Some have urged that our own courts ought to follow their example and emphasize reconciliation rather than the breach of law. Nevertheless, in most of the new African countries and in New Guinea at the present time, officially recognized local courts appear to be shifting more and more toward the position that disputes and offenses ought to be dealt with in an impersonal fashion, emphasizing the case, rather than the disputants. Under regulations now followed by local courts in Zambia, a plaintiff may not introduce testimony on matters not covered in his original complaint on which the summons was issued, nor may the defendant seek to extenuate his behavior by describing previous episodes in which the plaintiff has injured him. They are told not to return again to old battles, but to stick to the present issue.

The African political elite who press forward reforms in the court system appear to favor the restriction of the right of the court to probe relationships and also the development of a codified law that reduces the discretion of the court. Their policy, no doubt, is based upon a variety of considerations besides the belief that an impersonal code is more equitable and easier to administer. Burton Benedict (personal communication) has suggested to me that the policy may reflect a local demand for what people have come to regard as an alternative system of handling disputes, valued by them precisely because it operates in a different fashion from the local system with its emphasis upon the mesh of social relationships and the assessment of character. In deciding which to use, litigants assess the particular advantages of each system against its disadvantages. One advantage seen by some is the possibility for corruption once the court is no longer controlled by local opinion and is subject to review only by those in higher echelons of the legal and political systems (Shack, 1969: 164–65). But there is more involved than local pressure for an alternative system. Later in this chapter I shall argue that "tradition," declared and upheld in the courts or by local gatherings has been a powerful check on the extension of the controls of a central authority. The political elite of the new Africa appear to be aware of this possibility. They minimize the ability of the courts to check the central power by restricting them to a narrow consideration of particular cases and so give them little opportunity to formulate local usage.

Controls on Power: Tradition and Legality

I have argued that people with highly egalitarian institutions may have been willing to cede something of their independence to obtain a kind of security, although this may have been because they did not know the ultimate costs and thought they were welcoming an ally rather than a ruler. Like the rest of us, once under authority, they face new problems. They want to control the new power in their own interests. They also learn that they must now defend themselves against those who represent the power of the state and that this supersedes the old necessity for vigilance against one's neighbors. Morgan recognized this fact and indeed saw much of political history as a struggle between the representative council, regarded by him as the embodiment of the general interest, and the executive, which sought to extend its role and entrench itself to the detriment of council and people. His position is not far from that of Dahrendorf, who argues that "institutions exist to protect men from the badness of their fellowmen rather than as monuments of consensus" and points out that "Power always implies non-power and therefore resistance. The dialectic of power and resistance is the motive force of history. From the interests of those in power at a given time we can infer the interests of the powerless, and with them the direction of change." (Dahrendorf, 1968: 148, 227).

Balandier, in *Political Anthropology,* also emphasizes that the creation or imposition of a superordinate authority engenders attempts to control or combat it:

> Ambiguity . . . is a fundamental attribute of power. In so far as it depends on a more or less accentuated social inequality and guarantees the privileges of those who hold it, it is always, though of varying degrees, subject to contestation. At the same time it is accepted (as a guarantee of order and security), revered (by virtue of its sacred implications) and contested (because it justifies and maintains inequality). All political regimes express this ambiguity, whether they conform to tradition or to bureaucratic rationality. (Balandier, 1970: 40–41)

But Balandier seems to regard the emergence of checks on power to be as inevitable as the contest when he writes, "power tends to develop as a relation of domination, but the consent that legitimizes it tends to reduce its control" (Balandier, 1970: 40). This last statement smacks too much of the old equilibrium model or of an era of social anthropology when it often was assumed that a social order, or a culture, must be acceptable because it existed. The struggle to restrict the impingement of superordinate power is carried out more consciously.

Aside from outright resistance, those involved in the struggle have two principal means at their disposal: an appeal to tradition and a rigorous attention to legality.

We have come to think of the first as a conservative entrenchment of conditions being rapidly outmoded, although under some circumstances it becomes a principal tool used by those who wish to run their own affairs and follow their own lines of development. We are also inclined to think of rules as restrictive to the public, rather than recognizing that the rigorous expectation that officials must live by the rules they enforce is a primary safeguard against the arbitrary exercise of power.

Our thinking about the role of tradition inevitably has been affected by Max Weber's concept of an ideal type of "traditional authority" in which "legitimacy is claimed first and believed in on the basis of the sanctity of the order and the attendant forms of control as they have been handed down from the past, 'have always existed' " (Yalman, 1973: 139). As Nur Yalman has recently pointed out, Weber's use of the term traditional assumes that the critical element is continuity with the past. Anthropologists, however, have found traditional rules being invented on the spot to legitimate a course of action desired by very realistic manipulators of the local scene.

Again our best information here comes from fieldwork in Africa. Prior to the development of African political parties, and perhaps also in recent years since one-party and military regimes have come to dominate so many of the new African states, local attempts to restrict and control the authority of the central power were usually implicit rather than explicit because citizens could not rely upon overt legal regulations. Attempts to control colonial officials, including chiefs and others co-opted into the administrative structure, or to use the power of such persons for individual or sectional interests, went on through channels in which no one found it expedient to formulate how the process worked (see for example, Sangree, 1966: 131–35). Rules that existed for the control of arbitrary use of power by administrative agents were usually of little direct use to the people governed because the rules themselves were formulated at the administrative center and were not publicized locally. Furthermore, channels were not provided through which people could complain against tyranny or insist that an administrator and his agents be brought to book for breaking rules. Real constraints on the power of colonial officials, who attempted either to force change or to interfere with certain kinds of changes, were informal in that they could not be phrased as institutions regarded as part of the formal apparatus of government. Large spheres of activity in a sense were sealed off from administrative action by the recognition that people had their own systems for regulating their lives: administrators could act within these spheres primarily in their role of an appeal court with the right to review cases or to hear disputes which could not be settled locally.

John Barnes was among the first to call to our attention the fact that during the colonial period, innovation from the grassroots was typically introduced under the guise of tradition. The colonial administrations assumed that legislation was the prerogative of the central power and was legitimate only if carried out under its direction and on subjects dictated by it. The people had the right to live as their ancestors had done, if this did not conflict with colonial policy, but did not have the right to create independently as they came to query the utility of existing practices. The astute therefore legitimated the new with an appeal to tradition, on which they and not the agents of the central power were the recognized authorities (Barnes, 1951). Instead of going to the district administrator to ask if they might do something, they said, "This is what we have always done."

Given the fact that colonial governments were not prepared to divert sufficient resources into local areas to allow for large-scale experimentation with new economic and social institutions for which they could take credit, they had to assume that life was being led by old routines and under forms of organization on which the local people were the acknowledged experts. If people wished to refuse compliance with an administrative directive, the most effective plea was that it ran counter to tradition, especially if religious sanction was claimed for the tradition. This meant that the central administration had to consider the consequences of forcing people to commit sacrilege.

Barnes noted that under the circumstances, the interaction between law and politics was close and direct and that the courts which were assumed to operate in terms of customary law became major political institutions through which policy was determined and innovations implemented. Barnes writes from experience among the Ngoni of eastern Zambia and central Malawi, once rulers and subjects of a powerful state, but his observation probably also applies to areas occupied by egalitarian peoples after the newly instituted courts had been in operation for more than a few years. It rests upon the dichotomy of experience between those who live within the community and can be assumed to know its ways and those who occupy the upper echelons of power who are neither drawn from the community nor live within it. Inevitably the latter are sealed off from local knowledge vital to the running of ordinary activities and the information they receive is carefully controlled. Barnes comments,

> The virtual absence of legislation entailed lawmaking by the court, particularly in times of rapid social change. The judges were men of power and influence enjoying the patronage of their chief and hence were well qualified to sense the strength of public feeling and to carry through a ruling when once it had been made. Laws and precedents were not recorded, and the manner in which they were remembered and used was determined by present interests, principally by the interests of those in power who controlled the operation of the courts. Because the court members were not only judges, but also councillors and village headmen, they had an interest in good administration and in social development, in *order* as well as in *law*. Hence they tended to examine all the social implications of the specific dispute that was brought before the courts, ranging widely in their cross-questioning, and tried to find a solution which in many, though not all cases, reconciled the parties and at the same time upheld recognized rights. (Barnes, 1969: 113)

As we have seen, the ability of the court to innovate under these circumstances may lie behind the attempts of the new political elite to restrict them to matters of fact rather than to an adjudication that establishes the rules for appropriate behavior. The elite are attempting to channel policy and policy decisions through the political party and the upper levels of administration and are prepared to undercut the claim of local people to an exclusive knowledge of what ought to be.

The necessity of presenting one's case in terms of tradition, when final decisions are to be made by those outside the local system, has consequences which anthropolgists have not sufficiently explored. Political struggles for the control of the local scene and various attempts to influence higher echelons of government had to be fought in terms of rules alleged to have existed in the past. Some of the ambiguities in the rules described by Gluckman, Turner, and others who have concerned themselves with problems of conflict may well be the result of just this situation: local people could not meet and decide what it was they wanted to do in terms of the current situation because someone higher up would insist on a definition of why they had the right to do it that way. Men had to cite precedent to justify their demands and necessarily, therefore, they invented precedent. The totality of rules adduced *had* to conflict because they were invented to justify competing claims, as Werbner has so convincingly shown in his reanalysis of the arguments put forward by claimants for the Bemba kingship (Werbner, 1969). The situation also made it appear that people were much more bound by rule than in fact they may well have been and minimized their willingness to change. Yet in fact, anthropologists have stressed the flexibility and fluidity of customary law and procedures, so long as these were not reduced to writing, a fate that overtook the Adat law of Indonesia and created enormous problems in the latter days of Dutch rule.

Heesterman, who writes of the Indian village panchayat, or council, finds the same flexibility and fluidity referred to by writers on African courts. He argues that this flexibility and fluidity were based on

> the intuitive understanding that the participants in the face-to-face society have of the web of social relations and each other's place in it. This intuitive knowledge makes it possible to do without objective rules, precedent, and case construction and yet arrive at decisions (or stalemates) that are acceptable to the participants. But the results from case to case will often be far from lucid to the outsider, let alone easily comparable. For customary law and its proceedings are not concerned primarily with the objective truth of the matter but with the subjective truth of the persons involved which will differ from situation to situaiton. Obviously, the worst thing that can happen to customary law is codification. And the same goes for the sometimes hair-raising complications of rights in the soil, the division of its produce, and even of weights and measures, complications that hardly seem to bother the local participants but only come out when the revenue administration wants to describe and fix them in an objective and systematic fashion. (Heesterman, 1973: 97–98)

Although Heesterman does not say so, one reason why the codification of customary law has consequences undesired by the community is that it makes it possible for the outsider to become an expert on the rules that ought to apply within the community and so to gain control of the activities of its members in a new fashion. It is not merely the fact that the codification makes for rigidities in the law as operated by the local people. They, after all, could handle the code as we do our Blue Laws, or the legislation of university senates, invoking them only when it seems expedient to use them to obtain some objective not handled by an existing consensus. A code in the hands of a foreign administrator who assumes that it means what it says becomes an instrument of repression and a foe to the imaginative innovation which can go on only so long as the local people are the sole repositories of the legitimizing tradition. Their innovation has to stand the test of popular approval, or at least the mobilization of strong support, but that is determined by the effectiveness of the innovation in dealing with the current situation, rather than by its faithfulness to a dimly remembered and not necessarily honored past.

Ambiguity is an important aspect of the political process, as Balandier said, since it allows for adaptation. This has made it no easier for the anthropologist, and perhaps explains some of his unpopularity in areas where he has made his greatest contribution to our knowledge of the workings of social systems. If the anthropologist concentrates upon the formal aspects of political and social structures and so produces codes, that is, abstract statements of the rules people say ought to be observed, he is an enemy to the maintenance of the flexibility needed to allow those operating the system to fight their battles and make the compromises they deem desirable. He provides the tools that allow the foreigner to become an expert on local usages and so assume the right to arbitrate in local affairs.

If the anthropologist attempts instead to describe the dynamic processes by which the community adjusts to changing circumstances, he concentrates upon particular political battles. This entails exposing the stratagems employed by particular persons to give an aura of respectability to an otherwise completely implausible narrative. It is perhaps not surprising that so many of our contemporaries have retreated from trying to deal either with events or with rules of procedure and have turned instead to concentrate upon symbolic systems. These by definition are assumed to be impersonal, above the battle, and to operate by their own logic.

The appeal to tradition to legitimize behavior fails in situations where people begin to experiment with living conditions that are patently new. In these cases, there is no way to elevate local authority over the authority of representatives of the central government in the struggle for control. During the colonial regime, this left those who migrated to the towns and cities of Central Africa, as well as those who entered employment in industries and plantations, without effective tools for defending themselves against officials and employers because both cities and industry arrived with the colonial period. This made it difficult to operate local systems of adjudication in the cities or on plantations independently of the officials. Colonial officials assumed that they themselves were the experts on the situations which they believed Europeans had introduced. Insofar as such situations were to be governed by tradition, they and not the local people were the repositories of tradition. Colonial administrators and European employers were freed effectively from controls stemming from the local population other than those based on the threat of rebellion or the withdrawal of work. In the towns it became necessary to argue one's rights in terms of legal rules based on legislation or of values stemming from the metropolitan countries.

Inevitably this led to a struggle to control legislation and to write the terms of contracts, and so to the political party and the trade union. Members of the rising political elite also found that it was necessary to establish alliances with members of the metropolitan area through whom they could appeal arbitrary actions of local colonial administrators who had arrogated the right to judge how well they themselves conformed to the official standards appropriate to their roles. When the new political institutions created in the towns linked with the people of the countryside, the latter, too, found a way to bring district officers and other local colonial representatives under the scrutiny of public opinion and could enforce upon them some kind of compliance with the legal rules already in existence to delimit their power. For a brief period it became very important what people thought about their government and the way it impinged upon them; the representatives of that government became in a real sense public servants rather than servants of the state. It was also noticeable in the rural areas during that period that people were less apt to couch an explanation of their behavior through an appeal to tradition and assumed rather that they had the right to make decisions that took into account their appreciation of the current situation and their hopes of the future (Colson, 1967).

For a variety of reasons, tradition has never had the same legitimating force in the United States that it has had in colonial regimes elsewhere in the world. An appeal to tradition against impinging authority, of course, is effective only if those in authority are prepared to recognize the validity of other ways of life. It was a highly effective device in British colonies which were administered by officials who came from a country with a long tradition of common law, a respect for inherited position, and dominated by a Burkean belief in gradualism. It had less force in French colonies. It had almost none in the United States with its policy of cultural assimilation where effective power was in the hands of upholders of a particular tradition to which others were expected to conform. In Africa, therefore, we find local communities legislating under the guise of an appeal to tradition and also keeping at bay attempts to foist new programs upon them by arguments that the programs were alien to their traditions. American Indians had no such resource in their attempts to maintain some kind of control over their own destinies, for they were administered by those who regarded Indian institutions as both inferior and a barrier to the desired assimilation. Struggles for local control or for the containment of the power of the Bureau of Indian Affairs or other governmental agencies, therefore, have been based usually on an appeal either to treaty rights or to general rights formulated in the American constitution: rights to religious freedom, freedom of government, freedom of speech, the right to representation.

Frank Miller's account of a factional battle on a Chippewa reservation is very apropos of the irrelevance of any appeal to a legitimacy based on tradition, given American attitudes. The battle was over control of a council, recognized as the official local government body by the Indian Service and other agencies of the Federal and State Governments. One of the factions appealed to one set of traditional rules; the other appealed to a different tradition. According to Miller, "The committe of inquiry recommended that neither council be recognized, and that the tribe adopt a new constitution that would establish a more adequate and less ambiguous form of government." (Miller, 1966: 184–85).

We find American Indians facing the same difficulties whether they have attempted to protect old institutions or to innovate. An appeal to tradition has been ineffective under most administrations and in most circumstances. The contrast with the colonial situation elsewhere in the world emerges clearly in the sphere of religious innovations. During the colonial era in Africa, people were usually free to follow what religion they would, much as they would, so long as they claimed to be worshipping as their fathers had done, though certain religious practices might be suppressed as contrary to natural law. Missionaries might attempt to use the civil authorities to help them in their proselytizing, but by and large civil authorities did their best to prevent both missionaries and their converts from forcibly disrupting traditional worship. At the same time, they protected the right to worship in the new fashion. Local innovations in ritual were possible and even new religious movements, unconnected with the mission churches, might arise and spread throughout the country so long as their leaders took the precaution to phrase their ritual and theology in what were assumed to be indigenous terms.

But those who attempted to found new independent churches were immediately suspect and their churches viewed as an impingement upon the sphere of the administration and the missions. They were required to register. Very likely they were suspected of being subversive movements because they dealt with things belonging to the Europeans and assumed the right to transform social life, but yet did not accept European direction or the European as the final authority on dogma or ritual. They were therefore seen as disguised political movements and challenges to the established order. Official reactions to Kimbanguism, Kitawala, John Chilembe's church, or to Alice Lenshina's Church of the Women, were stronger than to a variety of other movements, such as the Mcape, which were not couched in Christian terms (Meebelo, 1971: 133–85; Shepperson and Price, 1958; Marwick, 1950; Richards, 1935).

Precisely the contrary situation prevailed in the United States until recent years. American Indians were not assumed to have the right to worship in some particular fashion on the grounds that this was their traditional form of religion. Nor could religious innovation be legitimized by using a traditional vocabulary or by arguing that it had ancient roots in the past. Indians found they could protect their right to worship in their own way by creating religious organizations that could acquire charters as churches under American law. Then, and only then, were they entitled to claim the privileges of religious freedom guaranteed by the American constitution. Traditional religion was regarded as superstition and therefore not entitled to legal protection. Peyote worshippers of the Plains and Shakers of the Northwest Coast learned to phrase their religions in such a way as to meet the requirements for a church and, once their members could produce a charter, the Indian agent could no longer disrupt their services and arrest those who persisted in attending. More recently, Indians are having to appeal to the courts for protection of their right to worship as they would against Indian councils, now recognized as the ruling bodies on reservations; these claim the right to control religious services and restrict the entry of new practices, whether they be fundamentalist Christian churches or the Peyote church. Their adherents claim their right to freedom of worship under the federal constitution.

The legalism of American Indians and the traditionalism of Africa appear to be striking reversals to the ethnographic accounts from the two regions, as Alfred Harris has verbally pointed out to me. Ethnographies on Africa stress the interest in jurisprudence, the emphasis upon legal arguments related to a view of man as governed by a social order to whose rules appeal is made. This is as true among most of the egalitarian peoples as it is among those who were ruled by kings and princes and took their cases to the royal courts. When the Tonga speak of *mulao,* which they translate as "law," they mean the rules that men should observe, but they recognize that the rules may be laid down by the central administration, by the courts, or by a man for the governance of his own homestead.

In the ethnographies dealing with American Indians, on the other hand, the people are shown as philosophers dwelling upon the intricate relationships between mankind and divinities described in myth, with the ancient exploits of divine beings seen as a guide to the human condition. This may be, as William Shack has suggested to me, because Native American political and legal institutions had been largely destroyed before the ethnographers reached the reservation, and that frequently they worked with older informants who were retreating from an involvement in the tragedy of total defeat into a world of myth.

But it is also true that the denial of any local autonomy to Native Americans on their reservations gave them less reason to update their traditions of law and order and so connect past with present (Bruner, 1973: 228–30). Instead, they were forced to defend themselves in alien courts which were governed by legal rules stemming from another tradition. They could neither withdraw from close supervision by their agents nor use the power of numbers to gain the political power that would affect federal and state legislation and obtain the passage of laws favorable to their own interests. Their ultimate tragedy has lain in the fact that the courts, which should have given them protection under existing laws, too often bowed to pressure from more powerful American white opponents who failed to see that ultimately the maintenance of their own rights under the law rested upon insisting that the Indians, and all others living under a common government, received their full measure of justice.

five

THE SEARCH FOR UTOPIA

Communes and other alternative communities find their safety in the existence of the state and its ability to maintain the public peace. They take their right to security for granted, in contrast to the egalitarian communities they emulate. People who lived in small face-to-face communities with no ultimate authority to which to appeal believed themselves exposed to the violence of their neighbors, and sometimes were. Self-restraint under provocation and vigilance to restrain kin and other associates were seen as essential in the face of the demands of the strong or the covert malice of hidden envy.

Where members of such communities have been unable to create a larger order with sufficient bite to restrain themselves and others, they have found new security, as well as hardship, in an incorporation into larger national units under centralized governments with courts, allocated responsibility for adjudication, and administrative officers empowered to enforce judgements. In the colonial states, however, local people commonly attributed the obligation of maintaining order to the aliens who ruled them. They did not have to face the knowledge that ultimately the maintenance of order rests upon all members of the state. They were able to take the larger peace for granted and address themselves rather to finding the means of restricting the further demands of the central power for control over their lives. Commonly they cited tradition as a justification for resistance.

With independence, the central government can no longer be defined as alien and those who now direct it claim a mandate from the people for the creation of better social orders. They have such support as they obtain because people believe that they are capable of changing the conditions of poverty, isolation, and self-dependence now found so irksome. There may be little consensus about how government should be composed, who should be in power, or how it should carry out its tasks. There is considerable agreement that government should exist and work for an improvement in the lives of ordinary men and women.

The ideal societies, for which citizens who have known life in small self-contained communities strive, are strikingly different from the utopian dreams put forward by so many discontented Americans and Europeans of the 1960s, or for that matter by many earlier seekers for a primitive Eden. We have distilled, from our own discomfort with what we are, a vision of the innocent and contented savage, living in simple amity with his fellows. William Irwin Thompson, in his humanistic fantasy, *At the Edge of History,* epitomizes this retreat toward Eden when he writes, "The historical recapitulation of the myth of original sin is seen in the fall from the unity and generalized charisma of the tribal community into the multiplicity and routines of civilized man" (1971: 118). But as I have argued, we cannot assume that men in such societies have confused what is with what ought to be or that they have wished to be what they were. The "generalized charisma of the tribal community" is a myth, not necessarily shared by members of small egalitarian communities, who see that life is sometimes good and sometimes bad and believe that somehow it could be better. They, too, try to transcend their order.

Some would say that the primary way they have done this in the past is through ritual, which provides a momentary alternative to ordinary life with its perplexities, but does not change the real social and material conditions that continue to generate the same satisfactions and discomforts. Victor Turner, in his Morgan Lectures (1969), has seen in ritual the vehicle for creating "communitas," that perfect world in which we know for the moment the expansion of ourselves into communion with others. This he contrasts with "societas," that divided world of ordinary routines where life is measured out in roles and statuses.

I, myself, am sceptical of the ability of ritual to produce this transformation if it is used consciously for this end. Men united to perform a ritual regarded as essential if the crops are to grow, or the hunt is to be successful, or illness is to be warded off, or the blessing of divinity is to be obtained, may indeed find communion in the ritual as they blend themselves to their common purpose. But if they come together hoping only that through participation they will discover their common interests, they are much more likely to be reminded of their reasons to quarrel. If men have used ritual to create order, if is because they have believed it to have enduring effects upon activities with which all were concerned. They have believed it possible to create a better existential world and have hoped to escape from the evils of their present situation. As Lewis Henry Morgan pointed out, societies change because men believe that it is possible to reform and that they have the right to do so.

In their planning for a better world, some have been guided by the belief that men must reform themselves to make life better, while others have believed that societies themselves must be reformed. I shall concern myself initially with the followers of the first point of view and only later turn to the true Utopians, who would renegotiate the social contract.

The Perfectibility of Men

We cannot assume that a single model of an ideal ordering of social life prevails in even the simplest of societies. Some of the dynamics of social life can be traced to attempts to implement various models seen as competing possibilities (Leach, 1954). Nevertheless, in societies with egalitarian institutions, under minimal or diffuse governments, there can be no such conflict about the good society as has existed among ourselves. Moreover, as we have seen in earlier chapters, those who think of a better way to order life which would give immediate advantage, have a good chance to implement their project through the normal processes of discussion and adjudication; in this way there is no need to stress the break with the past. The formal order never becomes sadly remote from the possibilities people perceive (e.g., see Pospisil, 1969; Bruner, 1973; Schwartz, 1973).

It may be for this reason that we are much more likely to be conscious of a dissatisfaction with the nature of men than we are of a dissatisfaction with the nature of society. Our techniques, however, which emphasize what men think their society ought to be, elicit ideal models and so contribute to the same effect. Nevertheless, in examining the ethnographic data on reform movements among Americans Indians and in Central Africa, I have been struck by the extent to which they stress the need for individual reform and purification.

Gluckman's formulation (1960) that, in nonindustrial societies, people rebel against their rulers to install better men when things go wrong rather than initiate revolutions to reform their societies, has been much criticized. By and large, however, it holds good, although it can also be asked how many western countries have undergone revolution since industrialization. In centralized systems, such as the African kingdoms, where rulers and their officials bore the burden of maintaining order, the slogan appears to have been "throw the rascals out." In more egalitarian systems, the reform of *all* is demanded, since the burden of order is assumed to rest with all. The individual is to be made to conform to the ideal standard of the good person. This again is in line with what we have seen of the systems of social control in such societies where the public interest centers on the assessment of character and reputation rather than on particular actions.

Perhaps the clearest examples of the attempt at perfecting social life by reforming the individual is to be found in witch-finding movements, recurrent phenomena in Central Africa for at least the last seventy years and probably well before that. They are based on the belief that life is perverted by witches and sorcerers who disturb both the natural and the social order because of their ambition and malice. The belief assumes a closed universe with a limited life force available to those within it. Those who seek to monopolize more than their appropriate share are enemies of the natural order and of their fellows. This clearly falls under what George Foster (1965) has called "a theory of limited good." He believed the theory characteristic of peasant societies, but it is now recognized as applicable to much of agricultural Africa and Asia, as well as within Latin America, and it becomes increasingly applicable in university circles in these days of declining resources.

Witch-finding movements are further characterized by a belief that the evil wishes of sorcerers and witches are empowered by charms or a detectable substance and that techniques can be found for detection and treatment of the evil-doers. When they have been forced to abandon their medicines and can no longer destroy life and poison society, then communities will live in peace and harmony; nature, too, will be bountiful. All medicines that advance the individual at the expense of his fellows will be abandoned and only those medicines that work for the general good will remain (Mair, 1969*a*: 160–79).

This is the recurrent dream of many Central African communities. It is still apparent even though men and women today increasingly blame misfortune and unhappiness upon the shortcomings of the state and the delinquencies of its officials, who are often said to work for their own interests. When the witch-finder has come and gone, the community that has sought his services finds itself once again facing much the same dilemmas, falling back upon much the same suspicions, recognizing that they remain much as before with the same ambitions and hostilities. This does not destroy the faith that a better life would be possible if only they could find some way to prevent ambition, covetousness, and pride from being armed with medicines and so empowered to harm. They see themselves as having failed this time because some among them have managed to retain possession of a medicine more powerful than those utilized by the witch-finder or have found ways to import new medicines from outside the purified community.

In the three decades during which I worked in Zambia, I have never been so fortunate or unfortunate as to be present during the period when a witch-finder was carrying out a general cleansing of a community. For my knowledge of what happens on such occasions, I have had to rely upon descriptions written by colleagues working elsewhere in Central Africa and on descriptions of Tonga friends. Tonga accounts show clearly how much hope they invest in the cleansing as the solution to current unhappiness. In 1957, I left the people of one Valley Tonga neighborhood, who were faced with a food shortage and had just been through a series of deaths of elders and children, eagerly awaiting word that a witch-finder then working in the Gwembe Valley was moving into their vicinity. As they murmured to one another about deaths, illness, and surfacing hostilities, their constant theme can be summed up as "Oh, if the witch-finder would only hurry!" In 1963, people of the same neighborhood were again waiting hopefully for the coming of a witch-finder and viewing with indignation the disappearance of some of the more prominent elders who had found pressing business elsewhere. In 1973, I found them engrossed in a four day prophylactic ritual, carried out under a woman prophet who said she hoped soon to obtain a government license so that she would be able to begin the exposure of the sorcerers.

If the witch-finding movements do nothing else, they maintain the belief that life could be better and they permit communities to crystalize their views about what it is that is preventing them from realizing their vision of a good society. If only *all* could be converted, then evil would be banished and the ideal world would come into existence (Mair, 1969*a*: 171–79). They differ from the Jesus movement now sweeping the United States in that the witch-finding movements deal with individuals as members of communities: individual redemption is not an end in itself, but rather communal reform through the reform of those who do evil. The witch-finding movements come and go, leaving little behind them by way of visible change, because they call for the realization of an ideal community rather than the creation of a new ideal. But then, neither was the witchcraft crisis of seventeenth-century New England a call for a new social dispensation. Rather it was interpreted as an encounter of individual Christians with the devil, the evils engendered by their activities to be eliminated by driving forth the devil and destroying those who had become his agents (Ziff, 1973: 242–49).

In the African witch-finding movements, if new rules are instituted, these are likely to be minor variants on old themes, dramatizing the personal style of the particular witch-finder. But occasionally a witch-finding movement is associated with a demand for more radical reform, and then, and only then, does it lead to the formation of new communities whose members seek to embody some special message and create a new formal order, which will make it impossible for the Old Adam to reemerge. Even then they assume the continuing existence of the preexisting state to maintain the rule of law and the flow of goods and people over a much wider area than that controlled by the community. They involve themselves with the larger unit as little as possible, but, if they are to survive, this means imposing upon themselves stringent restraints on behavior so that neither quarrels within the community nor with outsiders give occasion for the entry of officials of the larger unit.

A New Social Order: Utopian Dreams

Such a melding of a cure of evil with a new order occurred in Zambia with the founding of the Lumpa Church, or Church of the Women, of Alice Lenshina (Fernandez, 1964; Roberts, 1972; Rotberg, 1961; Taylor and Lehmann, 1961: 248–68). The Lumpa Church challenged first the colonial rulers of what was still Northern Rhodesia and then the claim of African political parties and the Zambian government to the exclusive right to determine the basic institutions through which a new postcolonial society was to be realized. Many of its members have been in exile since 1964 when they fled across the border to escape the attacks of the Zambian army upon their villages.

Much of the initial appeal of the Lumpa Church to many of its followers lay in its claim to be able to identify and reform the sorcerer. When I attended a Lumpa church service in Bemba country in northern Zambia in 1957, a great portion of the sermon dealt with the problem of medicine and the control of sorcery. The measures the Lumpa took to ensure control over their members to prevent them from reverting to the use of medicines meant inevitably the claim to a separate jurisdiction from which appeal could not be made to the official courts of the country. These last were expected to operate on the assumption that sorcery does not exist and under the law of the country that held an accusation of sorcery to be an actionable offense. The Lumpa Church created its own echelons of authority operating under rules also created by the Church. For these it claimed a different legitimizing basis than that underlying the institutions operating in nearby villages living under the old dispensation. Its members denied the right of representatives of the central government either to question and override the rulings of the church or to have the privilege of judging how well its leaders and the ordinary members performed in their new roles. Furthermore, the church claimed the right to proselytize and so to extend its rule at the expense of the representatives of the central order. Finally, it rejected the right of the central government to tax its members or to subject them to general regulations, such as the rules requiring school attendance.

The clash between the two regimes was inevitable, though it might have been less drastic if the Lumpa Church had not emerged at a time of political flux associated with the ending of colonial rule and the establishment of independent African states. Social and political boundaries were temporarily obscured or questioned. Claims to the right to lead were based on different and conflicting criteria. Party leaders encouraged people to ignore the order of chiefs and district administrators and to boycott the official local courts (Hall, 1965: 145–244).

In this power vacuum, the challenge of the Lumpa Church was only one of many; the order it could provide for its followers gave it a strong appeal, especially in those regions where people had seen themselves as part of a hierarchy of order derived from earlier kingdoms now incorporated in the new state. It also found adherents amid the political and social turmoil of the cities of the Copper Belt, although the majority of its converts, I believe, were emigrants from the same rural areas where the Lumpa had its greatest success.

If the Lumpa people had had to build their communities at a time of less political turmoil, the Lumpa leaders might have been less intransigent in their claims to autonomy and superiority. It is even possible that they might have achieved a *modus vivendi* with the emergent power structure of the new Zambia and created devices through which they could pay lip-service to the overriding authority of the state while yet exercising the privilege of experimenting with alternative communities. The ultimate ideals its leaders voiced were not overwhelmingly different from those of the new political leaders. Lumpa leaders were linked to the new political elite by many ties—including kinship, clanship, and shared childhood experiences in the same villages, schools, and sometimes local churches. They had also shared the humiliations and deprivations associated with subordination to Europeans in the colonial state.

But the Lumpa Church, with its claim to exclusive domination over its members and its withdrawal from the larger social world from which its members came, was not able to solve the problem of how to be in that world and not of it. It may be that the problem was insoluble on any terms that the Lumpa could accept, given what is now happening in Zambia and Malawi to the Watchtower, the African Branch of the Jehovah's Witnesses. The latter, of course, have frequently come into conflict with state and federal governments in the United States and with European governments because of their adherence to their own law, whether or not this conflicts with that of the larger political units within which the Witnesses also find themselves.

Watchtower was initially founded by missionaries who preached both personal reform and a new dispensation requring its own society. Converts were withdrawn from their old communities and encouraged to associate themselves only with others who had been saved, except for purposes of proselytizing. The Watchtower critique of the world was couched in stringent terms, and this brought its members into direct conflict with colonial officials, especially when they insisted that they bowed only to God and repudiated the rule of the unrighteous. This last also brought them into direct conflict with officially recognized chiefs who were the heirs of ancient African kingships.

But a compromise appears to have been reached well before the end of the colonial era, with Watchtower members giving nominal recognition to the rights of government and tokens of respect to such of its representatives as they necessarily encountered. At the same time they tried to live so scrupulously that they were unlikely to come in conflict with those neighbors who did not share their Watchtower affiliation and so would not be brought before the courts. They, therefore, avoided the question of jurisdiction, once they had agreed to pay taxes. They made no attempt to enter the political arena in any overt fashion, but instead devoted themselves to active work on their own economic enterprises and in behalf of their church and fellows in the church. Watchtower villages, scattered throughout much of northern and eastern Zambia and also in Malawi, have been recognized for many years as strongholds of the protestant ethic and models for neatness and prosperity. The ban on alcohol means that Watchtower members are unlikely to be present at beer drinks or other occasions where fights frequently break out. Few disputes from their villages ever reach the courts (Cunnison, 1951; Long, 1968; Meebelo, 1971, pp. 133–85).

Nevertheless, the Zambian newspapers during 1972 carried reports that the government was banning all Watchtower activity that might lead to an increase in membership. They might no longer go from house to house, distributing literature and trying to attract people to the church. They might not hold public meetings to which outsiders might come. They would be permitted to meet in their own homes and in closed church services, but any indication that they were trying to extend their sphere of action could bring a total ban upon them. Apparently the Zambian government is prepared to accept the barriers to its overriding claim upon Watchtower members as citizens of Zambia and to recognize their right to live according to the standards of their exclusive society only so long as Watchtower understands that it cannot extend its sway and does not attempt to impose its own vision of the ideal society upon the world at large.

The witch-finding movements may challenge particular incumbents or power positions momentarily, and usually only those of the lowest echelons of the hierarchy. They pose no such threat as the Lumpa or Watchtower to the social cohesion of the larger community because they project no alternative vision of what society should be. They only say that men should be good in such a society as they have.

Once, they may have put in question the belief that government must be based upon a general consensus about the nature of society and the purposes of men and administer laws derived from this consensus. But that was during the colonial era when the aliens who controlled the central government and the majority of the people who lived under the government held very different views about the way power flows from things to persons, from persons to things, and from person to person. Even then, witch-finders and the believers in them did not attempt to create new systems of authority or new methods of negotiating conflicts of interest anymore than they do at the present time when communities may publicly summon a witch-finder and are not concerned to hide his visit and their own activities to prevent any clash with officials of the central administration. At the present time witch-finding ceremonies are even less likely than during the colonial era to raise fundamental questions about the nature of social life and the content and source of law. They are therefore permitted to persist. I am not aware of any current attempts being made to regulate them; rather, I have been told that particular witch-finders have used the courts to sue delinquent clients who have failed to pay for services rendered. In the one case heard in a court while I was present which seemed to fall into this category, the court held that plaintiff and defendants had entered into a contract, that it was immaterial what the contract was about, that the plaintiff had fulfilled his part of the bargain and that the defendants were liable for breach of contract.

Even though they may now ply their trade openly, the witch-finders fail to achieve a permanent improvement in the texture of local life. This goes on as before. They do not diminish the ultimate dissatisfactions of the members of communities which attempt to use them. Some of those dissatisfied try to escape the recurrent dilemmas by joining new religious communities such as the Lumpa, before it was banned, or the Watchtower, and so subject themselves to a different regime seen as permanent. Many more try to escape by moving to the cities or to other rural areas where they hope for better things. If you cannot reform the sorcerers at home, at least there is the hope that you can leave the sorcerers and critics behind and find more congenial companions with whom to lead the good life. Some join political parties and work within them to try to implement programs of development that will change local conditions, under the expectation that education and prosperity will reform society.

The migrants' immediate solution seems linked to the belief

that life will be good if one can associate with good people. The flight need not be linked with a radical querying of the overarching structure of society. This may be taken for granted, as indeed it seems to have been taken for granted by many of those who escaped to the Left Bank or to Greenwich Village or to San Francisco and Berkeley, seeking the "ideal others" rather than dedicating themselves to the hard labor of creating the ideal society. This is not to deny the existence of Utopian builders among those who have migrated. I am merely pointing to the fact that making the scene carries no necessary commitment to accepting the consequences of revolutionary action.

The New Social World

In Africa, those who are escaping from the close-knit social networks of village society, with all the constraints these entail, to move into what they hope is the more impersonal world of the cities, are helping to transform their societies and to build modern nations even though they themselves may have no blueprints for Utopia. Such blueprints are more likely to be the property of intellectuals and political leaders. The ideological statements of these leaders frequently clash with the compromises people have made in their lives as, under the new conditions, they must work out both formal and informal rules and etiquette for dealing with one another. These new guidelines became necessary in cities where one can no longer expect to have an intimate knowledge of the majority of those with whom one interacts and cannot predict behavior from character.

Those moving to the cities, and indeed those at home who are increasingly exposed to pressure from the central government and its agencies, need to find and formulate categories broad enough for sorting and identifying those they encounter. They are also looking around for methods of interpreting, and so predicting, behavior. Like the rest of us, they want to know what they will risk by investment in particular encounters. In Africa, as a heritage of the colonial period, central governments have a greater impact upon their populations than is the case in many western countries, including the United States, because of the general lack of private capital for development and the relatively minor role of private enterprise. Most of the people in the cities, as in the countryside, have only very generalized skills and move from one unspecialized job to another, rather than pursue particular careers whose requirements provide a basic focus for social identification. The opening of many jobs to local people came as a result of political struggle rather than through the demonstration of technical skills.

The concatenation of these circumstances has led to a disconcerting increase in the emphasis upon ethnic identities even as people more and more come to share a common culture, and in direct conflict with the official ideology that emphasizes a common national citizenship. Many foreigners, and some African political leaders, have seen the emphasis upon ethnic labels as a recrudescence of ancient parochial loyalties and have attributed it to the weight of tradition. From it they have diagnosed a lack of commitment to the new political order of the nation state. In fact, most of the so-called "tribalism" that bedevils African life at the present time is a recent growth and brought about by the same forces that gave rise to European nationalism in the nineteenth century and, no doubt, are now responsible for the increasing importance of ethnic politics in the United States. The same factors seem to underlie the rise of caste associations in Indian cities since the latter part of the nineteenth century (Bailey, 1963). These can be summed up in terms of the growth of the state and the intrusion of its agents into local communities and into spheres which were formerly assumed to be in the control of the individual.

In Africa, at the moment, people have good reason to be

highly conscious that important decisions are being made that will affect their most intimate destinies: what they will speak, where they may live, what opportunities will be open to themselves and their children. They have every reason then to try to ensure that someone sympathetic to themselves shall make the decision and to urge such claims as they have to special consideration. In the present context of African life, this is likely to mean that they look to someone with whom they can identify on ethnic terms. Each such appeal to one who comes to be identified as an "ethnic spokesman" encourages others to mobilize behind leaders identified with them in a similar fashion.

Africa is being troubled by the thrust of the emergent "ethnic groups" precisely because she is engaged in large-scale modernization and reorganization. A large number of new political roles have been created for which competition is theoretically unlimited. People can also now compete for old roles formerly preempted by colonial officials or by alien merchants and professional people (Mair, 1969*b*: 132). Occupants of the most powerful political roles are visible on a national scene rather than known as individuals by the mass of those upon whose lives they impinge.

In midcentury, observers of the growing towns of Central Africa noted that "tribalism" was the most important basis on which people categorized casual acquaintances and that identification in ethnic terms provided an immediate definition of the etiquette to be followed in any encounter (Mitchell, 1956: 43; see also Gluckman, 1960 and 1971*b*). The diversified population of the towns, drawn from many regions of Central Africa and Europe, was being conceptually organized under a few "ethnic" categories, easily learned and operated, much as the Tonga, as described in Chapter Two, had once used clan categories for organizing their population. Each "tribe" so recognized, including "the Europeans," was composed of people who in any other context would have thought of themselves as belonging to different ethnic units and would never have associated themselves together on any "ethnic" basis. "Tribalism" so called was being invented to carry out much the same function performed by clanship at an earlier period and a function which is still important in many parts of the countryside. Unfortunately, the new set of categories did not carry the stipulation of exogamy. Much the same process of creating new ethnic categories and then using them to mobilize populations for political purposes appears to have gone on elsewhere in Africa, as witness the growth of the so-called "tribal associations" in the cities of West Africa in the early decades of this century.

If political leaders are defined as casual acquaintances, as in a sense they are to most of those who know anything about them, then they are operating in the same kind of situation as the strangers who encounter one another in the Central African towns. Office gives one attribute by which people may identify each other, but in many contexts this serves only to publicize the fruits of office. The next most effective way of categorizing those encountered appears to be through some "ethnic" label that gives onlookers at least a preliminary basis for assessing how they will react and who their friends are likely to be. "Tribalism" then is an emergent feature of African society and though it is regularly denounced by African political leaders and intelligentsia, it is one of the constraints under which they must operate.

African political leaders and intellectuals who are attempting to create new models for African society oppose to "tribalism" and "elitism," their own theories of "African Socialism," "African Humanism," or "African Personality" (Meebelo, 1973; Nyerere, 1968; Zulu, 1970). Whatever the differences among them, such theories commonly stress a so-called traditional respect for certain aspects of human life that ought to be binding on legislatures, officials, and the populace at large. They are assumed to set the limits within which people must operate. However cynical the individual citizen or official may become as he compares practice with pronouncement, lip service to the officially promulgated values is expected as part of the etiquette of office and daily life. One can now be denounced for such un-African behavior as discourtesy, materialism, and the denial of the general rights of all citizens. It is emphasized that whatever the differences among them, they are all subject to basic common laws and benefit from the maintenance of the same order.

At the same time, the private citizen and the official alike are caught up in the struggle to find reasonable terms on which they are to deal with the mass of those they encounter. They cannot treat them as "universal man" any more than their ancestors could deal with those they encountered in a rural neighborhood without making distinctions among them. For many Africans working in the cities, "ethnic" categories provide the most useful primary distinctions and a first sorting of claims for assistance and support. They continue to operate in these terms despite official ideologies and their own agreement that "tribalism" is wrong, at least if used by their fellows against them.

The primary sort into ethnic categories is sometimes superseded by an appeal to loyalties associated with the growth of professional networks and residential networks. Both can be expected to become more important as employment stabilizes and cities become inhabited by people who have lived in long-term association and developed multiple ties to one another. Joan Vincent, for example, reports that the inhabitants of Gondo, a small town in Uganda, which has attracted immigrants from many parts of the country, "pride themselves on their non-tribal ethos if such considerations are forced upon them, claiming that the distinctive character of their community lies in the very fact that it is, indeed, made up of individuals from many backgrounds. They live together harmoniously and find it a better place for this very fact." (Vincent, 1971: 110). The people of Gondo stress that they interact with one another on the basis of sex, age, occupations, religion, politics, and prestige, as well as on the basis of ethnicity (1971: 258). David Parkin found much the same to be true in the section of Kampala where he worked in the mid-1960s (Parkin, 1969*a* and 1969*b*). As both point out, people operate with a number of different sets of categories and decide to which they will give priority according to particular situations, and thereby introduce a high degree of flexibility into their manipulation of their social environment. Vincent and Parkin were both dealing with long-established communities composed of relatively stable populations where people were concerned about their local reputations. Neighbors were controlled by expectations for future interaction as well as by the immediate advantages of their present encounters and therefore had the more reason both to trust one another and to exercise self-restraint.

How important this expectation of the future becomes in the context of the new African society is brought out by David Jacobson (1973) in his study of Mbale, another small Uganda city. In Mbale, Jacobson found two classes of townsmen: one composed of elite civil servants, who expected to be transferred from place to place as part of the regular pattern of their careers but to remain within the same governmental agencies; the other was composed of laborers who had no secure future in the town and therefore expected to return to the rural areas from whence they had come. Laborers tended to interact with people who came from the same rural areas as they themselves. They could expect to meet again in the rural area even if they never encountered each other in another town on the next migration to work. For them "ethnicity" appeared to be a primary value, but it was a value closely linked to an expectation of future meetings.

If they wanted to follow up a debtor they expected to be able to locate him. Behavior in town had its repercussions at home and people could expect their fellows to take cognizance of this when they interacted in town.

Civil servants, on the other hand, were much less obviously associating on "ethnic" terms. They worked and played with those whom they expected to meet again in other towns and rural areas of Uganda as their paths crossed and recrossed while they pursued their separate careers. They became their own reference group and developed common standards by which behavior could be appraised and reputations established. Because of the expectation of future meetings with others in a common network, who would be interested in what each was doing, they recognized the possibility of their associates pooling information, and the risks of failing to meet accepted standards. As we have seen in Chapter Three, this is a vital element in the working of informal systems of social control precisely because sanctions can be invoked against the defaulter. Jacobson found that for both laborers and civil servants "an expectation of future interaction lends credibility to present association, despite its recognized short-term duration. Their belief about interaction, over time, including the establishment, dissolution, and renewal of social relationships, serve to maintain social order within the urban context." (Jacobson, 1973: 11; see also 98–100).

At the present time, I suspect Jacobson's findings would hold good for much of Central and East Africa. Despite official ideologies, African society might be represented as composed of two strands or networks, both enclosed within the larger political order. The first is composed of a career elite, bound together by their common expectations of the future, with a distinctive style of life and a constraining social network linked to the bureaucratic organization of government. It is upwardly mobile and attempts to assert its vision of a society of civil servants subordinated to the government it serves as the general pattern towards which community life should be modeled. The elite are not yet a completely differentiated class, although they tend more and more to be separated from the other strand. The members of this second strand form the bulk of the population and see themselves primarily as organized in networks that encompass the people of a particular region and a diaspora in the cities and towns of the country.

Each strand or network depends upon geographical mobility for its maintenance, and the increasing ease of transport permits each network to be close-knit. In 1972 and 1973, while Dr. Thayer Scudder and I were in Zambia continuing our long-term study of Gwembe Tonga adaptation, we found each school holiday marked by the joyous arrival in the cities of school children from rural areas, descending upon relatives in town for assistance with school uniforms and a base from which to sample the pleasures of town life. At Christmas time and on other official holidays, the trains and buses were packed and hitch-hikers lined the roads as those working in the cities headed home to visit kin and friends in the rural areas or in other cities.

The two networks are recent developments. Most members of the elite network are the first generation to move into bureaucratic jobs. Cross-linkages therefore connect those in one network with members of the other. The linkages are largely dependent on such associations as the elite continue to maintain with rural areas and their acceptance of responsibility to assist kinsmen less fortunate than themselves. Increasingly they appear to be attempting to segregate their interaction with the latter from their interaction with those whom they associate in the elite network.

Each network is vulnerable to contemporary developments. If the private sector grows to the point where it can employ many of the elite or if the government decides against a policy of transferring personnel from city to city and district to district, the elite network will tend to disintegrate and reform into many smaller units with particular interests based on their economic and regional associations. Its members will no longer share a common vision of what society should be. If labor becomes stabilized in the cities, networks based upon expectation of reunion at home will disintegrate. With it will go many of the common interests that now link urban and rural areas when people expect to alternate between the two. The growth of a town-bred population, habituated to the striking inequalities of city life and often to the ugly competitiveness of the city slum, encourages alternative visions of how men should live with one another. Categories based on occupation, religious affiliation, school fellowships, and city terrain will become increasingly important.

African cities and towns continue to grow; in some of them long-settled populations have begun to identify themselves primarily as members of an urban community. The gap continues to widen between the models of the ideal egalitarian community—publicized as the guide of political leaders in their planning—and life as it is lived in the cities or, for that matter, in the increasingly diversified countryside. People complain of growing violence, of the increasing sophistication of organized crime, and sometimes of a lack of respect for established authority. They take crowd action against those caught in the act of theft; in the cities they try to develop neighborhood or ward associations to help them to pool information and identify suspects, even though these cannot be taken before the courts for lack of evidence. They are as likely to emphasize a lack of law and order and the inefficiency of the police as they are to complain of obstructive laws, political chicanery, or police corruption. Those with means hire private security guards to protect their property as they face the new era of insecurity. Others, with lesser means, try to finance the purchase or the building of houses in suburbs occupied by house-owners who are seen as stable members of the community and unlikely to resort to violence or to harbor criminals. Others are left in sections of the city where the insecurity is such that women fear to leave their apartments for more than a few minutes lest they return to find all their possessions have disappeared.

Conditions in the new countries are not regarded as utopian by those who live within them despite the utopian dreams on which they were founded. The current dissatisfactions may be of a different order from those endemic to the small-scale world of the countryside or to the old egalitarian communities which some of them knew, but they reflect the same human dilemmas. Ultimate security rests upon the creation of stable communities. These impose their controls upon their members and restrain them from acting as they would.

Much of the population of the Central and East African cities is composed of young people who have tasted the personal freedoms associated with an escape from the immediate presence of their kin and allies into the anonymity of city life. They have been able to explore new experiences and follow their own desires as they never could at home. But they have done so by putting themselves at risk. As they mature and examine their experience, they appear to be willing to subject themselves and their children to new restraints in a search for security. They are attempting to create stable local communities within the cities where tradition can again become binding upon themselves and their fellows, and where informal social controls based upon the value of reputation will again operate. They are also looking to the legislature and the courts to develop a common body of law encompassing everyone, without respect to ethnic affiliation, and impartially administered by agents who are servants of the wider community rather than of any special segments within it. This they see as providing the framework within which it may be possible to pursue particular advantages.

Neither solution rests upon a dedication to egalitarian values, except for the belief that all should be equal before the law. The possibilities of the enlarged economic and social order have made it possible to escape from some of the limitations of the old communities. As a result people recognize new villains and are no longer so apt to blame particular ills upon neighbors or kin who envy them success or are trying to drain away vitality to enhance their own resources. Sorcery is said to exist in the cities, but it appears to be diagnosed as disconnected attacks for particular purposes against unrelated persons rather than as a generalized menace to which all are exposed. I have heard of a witch-finder being summoned to purify the relatively cut-off community of a farm compound where all work under the same employer, or to an industrial compound in a small Zambian town occupied by employees of a single firm. I have never heard of one asked to purify a town neighborhood or ward, where people make their living in a diversity of ways and have no immediate way to compare their particular rewards. In town, and increasingly in the countryside, ambition is recognized as legitimate as well as the fact that different ways of reaching the same common goal of a good life may exist.

Where the goals appear to be very different, people may still come under attack when they do not conform to the general pattern, as witness the fate of the Lumpa Church and the recent threats against Watchtower and other exclusive sects. There is very little official tolerance for alternative communities or for those who attempt to organize their view of the world through sets of categories at odds with the official ideology. Argument about ideologies is seen as disruptive by the political elites now entrenched in power; there is no reason to think their opponents would disagree with this position. Their own blueprints may sketch a different Utopia but one equally rigid.

The majority of the population, like the majority of any population, are much more concerned to find individual or general solutions to particular ills of the moment—now that the fervor of the independence struggle has vanished—than they are to plan an ideal world or seek to reform the total system. African school children are being taught to venerate their countries. Their elders, however, who have lived through the colonial era and know both the creation of the new national units and the political struggle which gave them their present political institutions are more irreverent. They see both country and government as having been created by men working together because they could reach some agreement about the ends they sought, but they regard the result as a compromise rather than a sacred heritage. They both attempt to evade and to use the official structures. They can be cynical about the motives and abilities of officials and political leaders and derisive about the official ideologies. But they do not want to live again in a world without a complex role structure, without free mobility, and highly developed economic institutions, without courts impartial at least by definition and other institutions of a developed governmental system designed to ensure a flow of goods and services and to maintain the public peace.

Like most of us, they do not want Utopia. They want good government and the honoring of the Social Contract.

REFERENCES

Ardrey, Robert

1971 *The Social Contract*. New York, Dell, 1971.

Bailey, F. G.

1963 "Closed Social Stratification in India," *Archives Europeene de Sociologie IV*, pp. 107–24.

1965 "Decisions by Consensus in Councils and Committees," pp. 1–20, in M. Banton, ed., *Political Systems and the Distribution of Power*. London, Tavistock.

1968 "Parapolitical Systems," pp. 281–94, in M. Swartz, *Local-Level Politics*. Chicago, Aldine.

1969 *Strategem and Spoils*. Oxford, Basil Blackwell.

Balandier, G.

1970 *Political Anthropology* (Translated from the French by A. M. Sheridan Smith). New York, Random House: Vintage Books.

Barker, Sir Ernest, ed.

1968 *Social Contract: Essays by Locke, Hume, and Rousseau.* (With an Introduction by Sir Ernest Barker). London, Oxford University Press. (First published 1947).

Barnes, J. A.

1951 "History in a Changing Society," *Journal of the Rhodes-Livingstone Institute XI*, pp. 1–9.

1969 "The Politics of Law," pp. 99–118, in M. Douglas and P. Kaberry, eds., *Man in Africa*. London, Tavistock.

Baxter, Paul

1972 "Absence Makes the Heart Grow Fonder; Some Suggestions Why Witchcraft Accusations are Rare among East African Pastoralists," pp. 163–92. in M. Gluckman, ed., *The Allocation of Responsibility*. Manchester, Manchester University Press.

Berndt, R. M.
1973 "Political Structure in the Eastern Highlands of New Guinea," pp. 381–424, in R. Berndt and P. Lawrence, eds., *Politics in New Guinea*. Seattle, University of Washington Press, 1973.

Berndt, R. M. and Lawrence, P., eds.
1973 *Politics in New Guinea*. Seattle, University of Washington Press.

Black, Jacob
1972 "Tyranny as a Strategy for Survival in an 'Egalitarian' Society: Luri Facts Versus an Anthropological Mystique," *Man N.S.*, Vol. 7, No. 4, pp. 614–34.

Bohannan, P.
1957 *Justice and Judgement among the Tiv*. London, Oxford University Press.

Bott, E.
1971 *Family and Social Network*. New edition. Glencoe, Free Press.

Brown, Paula
1972 *The Chimbu: A Study of Change in the New Guinea Highlands*. Cambridge, Massachusetts, Schenkman Publishing Company.

Bruner, E. M.
1973 "The Missing Tins of Chicken: A Symbolic Interactionist Approach to Culture Change," *Ethos*, Vol. 1, No. 2, pp. 219–38.

Burridge, K.
1973 "Tangu Political Relations," pp. 94–112 in R. Berndt and P. Lawrence, eds., *Politics in New Guinea*. Seattle, University of Washington Press.

Chagnon, N. A.
1968 *Yąnomamö: The Fierce People*. New York, Holt, Rinehart and Winston.

Chaney, W. A.
1970 *The Cult of Kingship in Anglo-Saxon England*. Manchester, Manchester University Press.

Chowning, A. and Goodenough, W. H.
1973 "Lakalai Political Organization," pp. 113–74 in R. Berndt & P. Lawrence, eds., *Politics in New Guinea*. Seattle, University of Washington Press.

Cohen, R. and Middleton, J.
1970 "Introduction," pp. 1–34 in R. Cohen and J. Middleton, eds., *From Tribe to Nation in Africa: Studies in Incorporation Processes*. San Francisco, Chandler Publishing Co.

Colson, E.
1953 *The Makah.* Manchester and Minneapolis, Universities of Manchester and Minnesota Presses.
1958 *Marriage and the Family among the Plateau Tonga.* Manchester, Manchester University Press.
1960 *The Social Organization of the Gwembe Tonga.* Manchester, Manchester University Press.
1962 *The Plateau Tonga: Social and Religious Studies.* Manchester, Manchester University Press.
1966 "The Alien Diviner and Local Politics Among the Tonga of Zambia," pp. 221–28 in M. Swartz, V. Turner, and A. Tuden, *Political Anthropology.* Chicago, Aldine.
1967 "Competence and Incompetence in the Context of Independence," *Current Anthropology,* Vol. 8, pp. 92–100.
1971 *The Social Consequences of Resettlement.* Manchester, Manchester University Press.

Colson, E. recorder and editor
1974 *Autobiographies of Three Pomo Women* (with introductory and concluding chapters and notes). Berkeley, University of California, Department of Anthropology, Archaeological Research Facility.

Cunnison, I.
1951 "A Watchtower Assembly in Central Africa," *The International Review of Missions,* Vol. XL, pp. 456–69.

Dahrendorf, R.
1968 *Essays in the Theory of Society.* London, Routledge & Kegan Paul.

Durkheim, E.
1947 *The Division of Labor in Society* (Translated by George Simpson). Glencoe, Free Press.

Easton, D.
1959 "Political Anthropology," pp. 210–62, in B. Siegel, ed., *Biennial Review of Anthropology.* Stanford, Stanford University Press.

Epstein, A. L.
1958 *Politics in an Urban African Community.* Manchester, Manchester University Press.

Evans-Pritchard, E.
1937 *Witchcraft, Oracles and Magic among the Azande.* Oxford, Clarendon Press.
1940 *The Nuer.* Oxford, Clarendon Press.

Feaver, George
1969 *From Status to Contract: A Biography of Sir Henry Maine 1822–1888.* London, Longmans, Green & Co.

Fernandez, J. W.
1964 "The Lumpa Uprising: Why?", *Africa Report,* Nov., pp. 30–32.
Firth, R.
1936 "Bond-Friendship in Tikopia," in L. H. Dudley Buxton, ed., *Custom is King*. London, Hutchinson.
Fortes, M. and Evans-Pritchard, E., eds.
1940 *African Political Systems.* London, Oxford University Press.
Foster, George
1965 "Peasant Society and the Image of Limited Good," *American Anthropologist,* Vol. 67, pp. 293–315.
Fried, Morton
1967 *The Evolution of Political Society: An Essay in Political Anthropology*. New York, Random House.
Friedenberg, E. Z.
1971 "Introduction," pp. 1–18 in E. Z. Friedenberg, ed., The Anti-American Generation. Chicago, Aldine.
Gluckman, Max
1955 *Custom and Conflict in Africa.* Oxford, Basil Blackwell.
1960 "Tribalism in Modern British Central Africa," *Cahiers d'Etudes Africaines,* Vol. 1, pp. 55–70.
1963 *Order and Rebellion in Tribal Africa.* London, Cohen and West.
1965 *Politics, Law and Ritual in Tribal Society*. Oxford, Basil Blackwell.
1971*a* "Preface," pp. xiii–xxx in E. Bott, *Family and Social Network*. New Edition, Glencoe, Free Press.
1971*b* "Tribalism, Ruralism and Urbanism in South and Central Africa," pp. 127–66 in V. Turner, ed., *Profiles of Change: African Society and Colonial Rule* (Colonialism in Africa, 1870–1960, Vol. III). Cambridge, Cambridge University Press.
1972*a* "Introduction," pp. ix–xxix in M. Gluckman, ed., *The Allocation of Responsibility*. Manchester, Manchester University Press.
1972*b* "Moral Crises: Magical and Secular Solutions," pp. 1–50 in M. Gluckman, ed., *The Allocation of Responsibility*. Manchester, Manchester University Press.
Gulliver, P. H.
1963 *Social Control in an African Society*. Boston, Boston University Press.
Hall, Richard
1965 *Zambia*. London, Pall Mall Press.
Hallpike, C. R.
1973 "Functional Interpretations of Primitive Warfare," *Man,* Vol. 8, New Series, pp. 451–70.

Hatanaka, Sachiko
1973 "Conflict of Laws in a New Guinea Highland Society," *Man,* Vol. 8, New Series, pp. 59–73.

Heesterman, J. C.
1973 "India and the Inner Conflict of Tradition," pp. 97–113 in *Daedalus: Post-Traditional Societies.* Proceedings of the American Academy of Arts and Sciences, Vol. 102, No. 1.

Hennigh, Lawrence
1972 "You Have to be a Good Lawyer to be an Eskimo," *Proceedings of the American Ethnological Society 1971,* pp. 89–109. Seattle, University of Washington Press.

Hobbes, Thomas
1968 *Leviathan.* (Edited by C. B. MacPherson). London, Penguin Books. (First published 1651).

Hocart, A. M.
1970 *Kings and Councillors: An Essay in the Comparative Anatomy of Human Society.* (New edition edited and with an introduction by Rodney Needham.) Chicago, University of Chicago Press. (First published 1936).

Hoebel, E. Adamson
1971 "Feud: Concept, Reality and Method in the Study of Primitive Law," pp. 1–15 in A. R. Desai, ed., *Essays on Modernization of Underdeveloped Societies,* Vol. 1, Bombay, Thacker & Co.

Howell, P. P.
1954 *A Manual of Nuer Law.* London, Oxford University Press.

Hsu, Francis
1973 "Prejudice and Its Intellectual Effect in American Anthropology: An Ethnographic Report," *American Anthropologist,* Vol. 75, pp. 1–19.

Hughes, Charles
1966 "From Contest to Council Among the St. Lawrence Island Eskimo," pp. 255–63 in M. Swartz, V. Turner, and A. Tuden, eds., *Political Anthropology,* Chicago, Aldine.

Jacobson, David
1973 *Itinerant Townsmen: Friendship and Social Order in Urban Uganda.* Menlo Park, Calif., Cummings Publishing Company.

Kaberry, Phyllis
1973 "Political Organization Among the Northern Abelam," pp. 35–73 in R. Berndt and P. Lawrence, eds., *Politics in New Guinea.* Seattle, University of Washington Press.

Kluckhohn, Clyde
1944 *Navaho Witchcraft.* Papers of the Peabody Museum of American Archaelogy and Ethnology, Vol. 22, No. 2.

Lawrence, Peter
1973 "Introduction," pp. 1–34 in R. Berndt & P. Lawrence, eds., *Politics in New Guinea.* Seattle, University of Washington Press.
1973 "The Garia of the Madang District," pp. 74–93 in R. Berndt and P. Lawrence, *Politics in New Guinea.* Seattle, University of Washington Press.

Leach, Edmund
1954 *Political Systems of Highland Burma.* London, Bell.
1973 "Buddhism in the Post-Colonial Order in Burma and Ceylon," pp. 29–54 in *Daedalus: Post-Traditional Societies.* Proceedings of the American Academy of Arts and Societies, Vol. 102, No. 1.

Locke, John
1965 *Two Treatises of Government.* (With an Introduction and Notes by Peter Laslett). New York, Mentor. (First published 1963).

Long, Norman
1968 *Social Change and the Individual.* Manchester, Manchester University Press.

Lowie, Robert
1927 *The Origin of the State.* New York, Harcourt, Brace.

Mair, Lucy
1962 *Primitive Government.* London, Penguin.
1969*a* *Witchcraft.* New York, McGraw-Hill.
1969*b* *Anthropology and Social Change.* (London School of Economics Monographse on Social Anthropology). London, Athlone Press.
1972 *An Introduction to Social Anthropology.* Second Edition. Oxford, Clarendon Press.

Malinowski, B.
1926 *Crime and Custom in Savage Society.* London, Routledge & Kegan Paul.

Marwick, Max
1950 "Another Anti-Witchcraft Movement in East Central Africa," *Africa,* Vol. 20, pp. 100–12.

Meebelo, Henry S.
1971 *Reaction to Colonialism: A Prelude to the Politics of Independence in Northern Zambia 1893–1939.* Manchester, Manchester University Press.
1973 *Main Currents of Zambian Humanist Thought.* Lusaka, Oxford University Press.

Merton, Robert
1972 "Insiders and Outsiders: A Chapter in the Sociology of Knowledge," pp. 9–47 in C. Arnold Anderson, ed., *Varieties of Politi-*

cal Expression in Sociology. Chicago, University of Chicago Press.

Middleton, John

1966 "The Resolution of Conflict among the Lugbara of Uganda," pp. 141–54 in M. Swartz, V. Turner and A. Tuden, eds., *Political Anthropology*. Chicago, Aldine.

1968 "Conflict and Variation in Lugbaraland," pp. 151–61, in M. Swartz, ed., *Local-Level Politics*. Chicago, Aldine.

Miller, Frank

1966 "Problems of Succession in a Chippewa Council," pp. 173–85 in M. Swartz, V. Turner, and A. Tuden, *Political Anthropology*. Chicago, Aldine.

Mitchell, Clyde

1956 *The Kalela Dance*, Rhodes-Livingstone Paper No. 27.

Moore, Sally Falk

1972 "Legal Liability and Evolutionary Interpretation: Some Aspects of Strict Liability, Self-Help and Collective Responsibility," pp. 51–107 in M. Gluckman, ed., *The Allocation of Responsibility*. Manchester, Manchester University Press.

Morgan, Lewis Henry

1870 *Systems of Consanguinity and Affinity of the Human Family*. Smithsonian Contributions to Knowledge, 17: pp. 4–602.

1962 *League of the Iroquois*. (New edition with introduction by William N. Fenton). New York, Corinth Books. (First published 1851).

1963 *Ancient Society*. (New edition edited and with an introduction and annotations by Eleanor Burke Leacock.) Cleveland and New York, World Publishing Company. (First published 1877).

Murdock, George P.

1971 "Anthropology's Mythology," *Proceedings of the Royal Anthropological Institute for 1971*, pp. 17–24.

Nader, Laura

1969 "Styles of Court Procedure: To Make the Balance," pp. 69–91 in L. Nader, ed., *Law in Culture and Society*. Chicago, Aldine.

Nyerere, Julius

1968 *Ujamaa: Essays on Socialism*. Dar-es-Salaam, Oxford University Press.

Parkin, David

1969*a* "Tribe as Fact and Fiction in an East African City," pp. 273–96 in P. Gulliver, ed., *Tradition and Transition in East Africa*. Berkeley, University of California Press.

1969*b* *Neighbors and Nationals in an African City Ward*. Berkeley, University of California Press.

Parsons, E. C.
1927 "Witchcraft among the Pueblos: Indian or Spanish?" *Man,* Vol. 27, pp. 106–12, 125–28.
Peters, E.
1972 "Aspects of the Control of Moral Ambiguities: A Comparative Analysis of Two Culturally Disparate Modes of Social Control," pp. 109–162 in M. Gluckman, ed., *The Allocation of Responsibility*. Manchester, Manchester University Press.
Pollard, Sidney
1971 *The Idea of Progress*. London, Pelican. (First published 1968).
Pospisil, Leopold
1969 "Structural Change and Primitive Law: Consequences of a Papuan Legal Case," pp. 208–29 in L. Nader, ed., *Law in Culture and Society*. Chicago, Aldine.
Radcliffe-Brown, A.
1940 "Preface," pp. xi–xxiii in M. Fortes and E. E. Evans-Pritchard, eds., *African Political Systems*. London, Oxford University Press.
Resek, Carl
1960 *Lewis Henry Morgan: American Scholar*. Chicago, University of Chicago Press.
Richards, Audrey
1935 "A Modern Movement of Witchfinders," *Africa,* Vol. 8, pp. 448–61.
Richards, Audrey and Kuper, Adam
1971 *Councils in Action*. (Cambridge Papers in Social Anthropology, No. 6). Cambridge, Cambridge University Press.
Roberts, Andrew
1972 *The Lumpa Church of Alice Lenshina*. Lusaka, Oxford University Press.
Rotberg, Robert
1961 "The Lenshina Movement of Northern Rhodesia," *Human Problems in British Central Africa,* Vol. XXIX, pp. 63–78.
Rousseau, Jean J.
1950 *The Social Contract and Discourses*. (Translated with an introduction by G. D. H. Cole). New York, E. P. Dutton. (First published 1762, 1755).
Sahlins, M.
1965 "On the Sociology of Primitive Exchange," pp. 139–236, in M. Banton, ed., *The Revelance of Models for Social Anthropology*. London, Tavistock.
Sangree, Walter
1966 *Age, Prayer and Politics in Tiriki, Kenya*. London, Oxford University Press.

Schapera, Isaac
1956 *Government and Politics in Tribal Societies.* London, Watts.

Schwartz, T.
1973 "Cult and Context: The Paranoid Ethos in Melanesia," *Ethos,* Vol. 1, No. 2, pp. 153–74.

Scudder, Thayer
1962 *The Ecology of the Gwembe Tonga.* Manchester, Manchester University Press.
1971 *Gathering among African Woodland Savannah Cultivators: A Case Study: The Gwembe Tonga.* Zambian Papers, No. 5.
1973 "The Human Ecology of Big Projects: River Basin Development and Resettlement," pp. 45–55 in Bernard Siegel, Alan Beals and Stephen Tyler, eds., *Annual Review of Anthropology,* Vol. 2. Stanford, Stanford University Press.

Shack, William
1963 "Religious Ideas and Social Action in Gurage Bond-Friendship," *Africa,* Vol. 33, pp. 198–208.
1969 "Guilt and Innocence: Problem and Method in the Gurage Judicial System," pp. 153–66 in M. Gluckman, ed., *Ideas and Procedures in African Customary Law.* London, Oxford University Press.

Shepperson, George and Price, T.
1958 *Independent African: John Chilembe and the Origins, Setting and Significance of the Nyasaland Rising of 1915.* Edinburgh, Edinburgh University Press.

Simon, Herbert
1972 "Cognitive Control of Perceptual Processes," pp. 91–109 in George V. Coelho and Eli A. Rubinstein, eds., *Social Change and Human Behavior: Mental Health Challenges of the Seventies.* National Institute of Mental Health, DHEW Publication No. (HSM) 72–9122.

Skinner, Elliott
1973 *Peoples and Cultures of Africa.* New York, Doubleday: Natural History Press.

Sorrenson, E. R.
1972 "Socio-ecological Change among the Fore of New Guinea," *Current Anthropology,* Vol. 13, pp. 349–84.

Southall, Aidan
1956 *Alur Society.* Cambridge, Heffer.

Southwold, Martin
1971 "Meanings of Kinship," pp. 35–56 in R. Needham, ed., *Rethinking Kinship and Marriage.* London, Tavistock.

Spalding, Francis O., Earl L. Hoover and John C. Piper
1970 " 'One Nation, One Judiciary': The Lower Courts of Zambia," *Zambia Law Journal,* Vol. 2, pp. v–xiv, 1–289.

Spencer, Herbert
1969 *The Man versus the State.* (Edited by Donald Macrae). London, Penguin. (First published 1884).

Spencer, Robert
1972 "The Social Composition of the North Alaskan Whaling Crew," *Proceedings of the American Ethnological Society, 1971,* pp. 110–20. Seattle, University of Washington Press.

Stern, B.
1931 *Lewis Henry Morgan, Social Evolutionist.* Chicago, University of Chicago Press.

Swartz, M., Turner, V., and Tuden, A.
1966 "Introduction," pp. 1–41 in M. Swartz, V. Turner and A. Tudens, eds., *Political Anthropology.* Chicago, Aldine.

Taylor, John V., and Lehmann, D.
1961 *Christians of the Copperbelt.* London, SCM Press.

Terray, Emmanuel
1972 *Marxism and 'Primitive' Societies.* (Translated by Mary Klopper, French edition 1969). New York, Monthly Review Press.

Thomas, Elizabeth
1959 *The Harmless People.* New York, Knopf.

Thompson, W. I.
1971 *At the Edge of History.* New York, Harper, Colophon Books.

Tuden, Arthur
1966 "Leadership and the Decision-Making Process," pp. 275–83, in M. Swartz, V. Turner, and A. Tuden, *Political Anthropology.* Chicago, Aldine.

Turner, Victor
1957 *Schism and Continuity in an African Society.* Manchester, Manchester University Press.
1966 "Ritual Aspects of Conflict Control in African Micropolitics," pp. 239–46 in M. Swartz, V. Turner, and A. Tuden, eds., *Political Anthropology.* Chicago, Aldine.
1969 *The Ritual Process.* Chicago, Aldine.

Van Velsen, J.
1969 "Procedural Informality, Reconciliation and False Comparisons," pp. 137–50 in M. Gluckman, ed., *Ideas and Procedures in African Customary Law.* London, Oxford University Press.

Vincent, Joan
1971 *African Elite: The Big Men of a Small Town.* New York: Columbia University Press.

Wallace, Anthony
1958 "The Dekanawidah Myth Analyzed as the Record of a Revitalization Movement," *Ethnohistory,* Vol. V, pp. 118–30.
1970 *The Death and Rebirth of the Seneca.* New York, Alfred A. Knopf.

Wallis, Wilson D.
1918 *Messiahs—Christian and Pagan.* Boston, R. G. Badger.
1943 *Messiahs: Their Role in Civilization.* Washington, American Council on Public Affairs.

Werbner, Richard
1969 "Constitutional Ambiguities and the British Administration of Royal Careers among the Bemba of Zambia," pp. 245–72 in L. Nader, ed., *Law in Culture and Society.* Chicago, Aldine.

Wilson, Godfrey and Wilson, Monica
1945 *The Analysis of Social Change.* Cambridge, Cambridge University Press.

Wilson, Monica
1971 *Religion and the Transformation of Society: A Study in Social Change in Africa.* Cambridge, Cambridge University Press.

Woodcock, George
1963 *Anarchism.* London, Penguin.

Yalman, Nur
1973 "Some Observations on Secularism in Islam: The Cultural Revolution in Turkey," pp. 139–68 in *Daedalus: Post-Traditional Societies.* Proceedings of the American Academy of Arts and Sciences, Vol. 102, No. 1.

Ziff, Larzer
1973 *Puritanism in America.* New York, Viking Press.

Zulu, J. B.
1970 *Zambian Humanism.* Lusaka, Zambia Publishing Company.

INDEX

Abelam, 40, 41
Academic life, 1, 4, 81, 93
Acephalous society, 66
See also Government, minimal and diffuse; Egalitarian societies
Action, 18, 51, 52, 53, 56
Accusations, 56–59
Adat Law, 80
Adjudication, 10, 14, 50, 53, 65, 69–74, 79, 82, 89, 92
See also Courts; Disputes
Administration, 3, 6, 27, 61, 79, 81, 83, 84, 86, 89, 101
colonial, 38, 39, 64–69, 70, 73, 77–80, 81, 82, 96, 99, 100
district, 3, 39, 67–68, 73, 78, 83, 97–98
structures of, 6, 77, 79, 80
See also Authority; Government; Bureaucracy; Officials
Adoption, among Iroquois, 20, 24, 28–29
African, 16–18, 28, 44–45, 64, 68, 70, 73, 74, 76–80, 84, 86, 102–113
Central, 3, 5, 7, 25–28, 82, 92–97, 104–113
East, 7, 57, 106–108, 111
West, 105
African humanism, 105
African personality, 105
African socialism, 105
African tradition, 8
African Political Systems, 14, 15, 17
Age sets, 26, 27, 70
Aggression, 33, 36–45
Agreement, 1, 14, 22, 25, 113
as contract, 10
trade, 24
See also Consensus
Alliance, 19, 20, 22, 30, 32, 37, 50, 59, 83
Allocation, right of, 52–53
Alternative communities, 1, 89, 96–102, 112

Alur, 64
Amazon Basin, 65–66
Ambition, personal, 15, 19, 28, 36, 48, 93, 94, 112
America, North, 65
South, 65–66
American, legal system, 54, 73, 86, 87
society, 35, 36–37, 58–59, 62, 84, 90
Anarchy, 3, 32, 34, 38, 62, 68
Ancient Society, xi, 4, 10, 11, 15, 23, 24, 28, 33
Anglo-Saxon, 21
Angola, 27
Anthropology, 2, 4, 11–19, 21, 22, 31, 33, 35–37, 52, 63, 66, 76, 79, 80, 81–82
American, 12, 13, 16, 36, 46
British, 11
Political, *See* Political, anthropology
social, 5, 14, 51, 76
Arbitration, 2, 64, 81
See also Adjudication; Disputes; Courts
Aristocracy, 17
Aristotle, 4, 14, 15
Arusha, 70
Assembly, popular, 9, 16, 33
representative, 10, 17–18, 69, 80
See also Council; Legislature
Assimilation, 26–30, 83–85
Assistance, 46–48
Association, 1, 26, 107–110
caste, 103
free-form, 1
men's, 16
neighborhood, 110
secret, 2
tribal, 110
Australia, 38, 40, 41, 64–45
Authority, v, 2, 4, 10, 13, 21, 31–36, 39, 56, 62–87, 89, 110
central, 66, 74, 77, 82, 98
claims to, 4, 78, 85, 97–98, 100
controls on, 4, 6, 61–87
dangers from, 6, 7, 33, 67
limits of, 61–87
respect for, 8, 64–69
sources of, 13, 21, 39
Autonomy, political, 2, 83

Bailey, F. G., 15, 18, 51, 103
Balandier, G., 75–76, 81
Band, 36, 43
Barnes, John, 77–79
Baxter, P., 57
Bemba, 27, 80, 96–97
Benedict, Burton, x, 74
Bentham, J., 10
Berndt, R. M., 7
Bias, legal, 71
Bilateral kinship, 16, 22
Black, J., 43, 67
Boas, F., 12, 16
Bohannan, P., 70
Bott, E., 55
Boundaries, political, 5, 22, 24, 28, 97
social, 5, 97
Brazil, 66
British, 35, 70, 83
Brown, Paula, 37, 38, 44, 65
Bruner, E. M., 87, 92
Bureau of Indian Affairs, *See* Indian Affairs, Bureau of
Bureaucracy, 7, 75, 108–109
Burke, Edmund, 83
Bushmen, 43–44

Captivity, 20, 24, 38
Career patterns, 107–108

Caste associations, 103
Categories, ethnic, 103–110
  social, 7, 8, 13, 19, 25–28, 29, 30, 57, 102–110, 112
Cayuga, 23
Central Africa, *See* Africa, Central
Ceremony, 28, 34
  See also Ritual
Chagnon, N., 66
Chaney, W., 21
Change, opportunity for, 7
  guarantees for, 63
  social, 11, 18–19, 62–64, 75, 77–84, 90, 91, 92, 95, 97, 98, 101
  See also Reform; Innovation; Experimentation
Character, importance of, 53–59, 74, 80, 93, 102
  See also Reputation
Charisma, 12, 90
Charismatic movement, 19,
  See also Messiah; Religious movements
Cherokee, 23
Chief, 33, 77, 79
  See also Leaders
Chimbu, 37–38, 41, 44, 65
Chilembe, John, 85
Chippewa, 23, 84
Choice, exercise of, 9, 10, 19, 43, 74, 91
  freedom of, 10, 74
  rational, 9, 11–13, 18
Chowning, Anne, 40
Church, new, formation of, 85–86, 96–100
Church of the Women, 84
  See also Lumpa Church
Civil service, 107–108
  See also Administration; Bureaucracy; Officials
Cities, conditions in, 7, 82, 98, 102–113
  law in, 83
  growth of, 7, 101, 102, 106–113
Citizenship, 7, 8, 103–111
Clan, 3, 5, 10, 16, 17, 20–30, 47–48, 98, 105
Class, social, 14, 15, 16, 26
  See also Elite
Clientship, 27
Codification of law, 80–81
Cohesion, social, 23
Colonial, period, 17–18, 38, 67, 77, 82, 100, 113
  rule, 3, 6, 17–18, 38, 39, 62, 66, 74–75, 77, 82, 84–85, 89–90, 96–97, 98–100
    See also Administration, colonial
Colonists, 11
Colson, Elizabeth, 40, 56, 68, 83
Command, hierarchy of, 2, 5
Communes, 8, 89
Community, 14, 15, 25, 51, 53, 66
  alternative, 1, 89, 96–102, 112
  face-to-face, 1, 4, 5–6, 50, 57, 73, 89, 102
  moral, 15, 18, 32, 36, 51, 94
  political, 15, 18, 21–22
  small-scale, 4, 6, 54, 59, 64, 111
  life-style, 6, 106–107, 110–113
  See also Society
Compensation, 53–54
Competition, 8, 14–15, 52–53, 70, 80, 104–105, 110
Compromise, 8, 33, 81, 113
  See also Adjudication
Conflict, 23, 36–51, 52, 63, 72, 79, 92, 97–100
Conformity, 7, 62, 71
Confrontation, 43–45, 71
Consanguinity, *See* Kinship

Consensus, v, 1, 5, 6, 7, 29, 31, 35, 51–59, 61, 75, 81, 90, 100
creation of, 6, 18, 54–59
role in maintaining order, 5
Consent, 12, 15, 34, 67, 76
Constituency, 20, 28
Constitution, 12, 84, 86
Constraint, v, 5, 15, 18, 30, 31, 35–51, 77, 100
See also Restraint
Continuity, 4, 5, 57–58, 76, 108
Contract, 1, 50, 83, 101
Contract, Social, v, 7–8, 10–13, 46, 81, 92, 113
Control, v, 33, 34, 66, 69
self, *See* Restraint
social, 4, 5, 6, 7, 14, 31–59, 61, 63, 69–74, 81, 82, 97–98, 108–113
means of, 4, 6, 53–59, 71–73, 82, 108
study of, 5, 31
Cooperation, 34, 35, 36, 45, 51, 57
Corporate group, 14, 24, 27, 30, 31
See also Associations; Councils; Descent groups
Corruption, 69, 74, 110
Council, 3, 10, 16, 17–18, 23, 31, 84, 86
clan, 10
Iroquois, 20, 41
See also Assembly; Legislature
Courts, v, 3, 4, 7, 10, 18, 51, 69–74, 77, 80, 86, 87, 89, 97, 101, 111, 113
corruption of, 74
as legislature, 78–81
powers of, 69, 72, 73
reform of, 73–74
Crime, 53–59, 110
Cross-cutting ties, 23
Culture, concept of, 12, 46
Cunnison, I., 99
Custom, 11, 51, 59
See also Tradition

Dahrendorf, R., 75
Damages, 72–73
See also Compensation
Decisions, community, 28, 29–30, 53–59, 80, 83, 104
implementation of, 6
See also Choice
Democracy, participatory, 3
theory of, 9
Descent, principles of, 23–24, 26, 28–29
Descent groups, 16, 19, 22, 27, 28,
See also Clan
Development, social, 79
stages of, 24
Discourse on the Origins of Inequality, 32
Discussion, importance of, 33, 53–59, 67, 92
See also Control
Disputes, 7, 14, 22, 37, 39, 40, 41, 43, 52, 79, 99
See also Aggression; Feud; Quarrels; Self-help
settlement of, 22, 43, 64, 69–74, 77, 79
See also Adjudication; Courts
Divination, 46
Domination, 13, 18, 33, 75–76
See also Authority; Control; Order
Durkheim, E., 12, 17, 23, 62

East Africa, *See* Africa, East
Ecology, importance of, 18, 57
Economic growth, 8
Education, 40, 43, 101, 113

Egalitarianism, 3, 8, 28, 31–59, 61, 62, 66–69, 70, 74, 78, 86, 89, 90, 92, 93, 110, 111–112
  See also Societies, egalitarian
Elders, 33, 40, 54, 55, 72, 95
Elite, African, 73, 74, 79, 105–107, 108–110, 112–113
  See also Leaders
Encroachment, 4, 33, 62, 75–84
  See also Authority; Domination
Enforcement, of contracts, 10, 40
  of law, 10, 72
    See also Law enforcement
Engels, F., 16
Envy, 38, 41, 44–51, 61, 89, 112
Equilibrium models, 76
Eskimo, 16, 41
Ethnic units and categories, 103–110
Ethnocentrism, 8, 35–36, 103
Etiquette, 25, 32, 102, 104–105, 106
Europe, 12, 54, 73, 98, 103
Europeans, 12, 21, 65, 90, 103
  in colonial period, 67–68, 82, 85, 98, 104
Evans-Pritchard, E. E., 14, 70, 117, 118
Evidence, 53–59, 69
Evolution, social, 24, 35
Evolutionists, social, 16, 19
Exchange, 20, 22, 45–46, 50, 51, 63
Executive, 5, 10, 14, 15, 17–18, 31, 33, 69, 72, 75, 76
Exile, 41, 42, 53, 96
Exogamy, 22, 105
Expectation, importance of, 2, 5, 42, 52–54, 57, 63–64, 108
Experimentation, 1, 63–64, 68, 78, 82, 98
  See also Change; Innovation
Factions, political, 19, 37, 84
Family, 34, 39, 63
  as model of political order, 1, 3, 20–21, 34
  patriarchal, 21
Father, power of, 21
Fear, 31–37, 55–56, 57–60, 63, 67–68, 89, 112
Feaver, G., 11
Fenton, W., xi
Fernandez, J., 96
Feud, 37, 41, 42–43, 70
  See also Self-help
Feudalism, 12
Field, political, 15, 18
  social, 6, 15, 18, 30
Fighting, 37–51, 64–69
  See also Disputes; Quarrels; Hostility
Firth, Raymond, 10
Force, use of, 36–51, 64
  See also Feud; Self-help; Violence
Fortes, M., 14
Forum, 72
  See also Assembly; Courts
Foster, G., 93
Freedom, 1, 4, 10, 66, 67, 71, 83–85, 111
  of action, 4, 42–43, 51–52, 72
  from encroachment, 4, 65–69, 84
  religious, 84–85
  See also liberty
Fried, M., 36, 37, 43, 44
Friedenberg, E. Z., 58
Friendship, 3, 53

Garia, 37
Genealogy, importance of, 22
Ghosts, 48–50, 56
Giving, 44–51, 53
  See also Reciprocity; Sharing

Gluckman, M., 5, 23, 43, 51, 52, 54, 73, 79, 92–93, 104
Goals, public, 15, 112
See also Consensus; Public opinion
Golden Age, 10, 32–33, 62, 65
Gondo, town of, 106–107
Good, general, 15, 19, 94
limited, theory of, 93
Goodenough, W., 40
Gossip, 54–59, 108
Government, attributes of, 5, 15, 31, 90
basis of, 10, 12
centralized, 2, 3, 5, 6, 7, 8, 15, 16, 34, 39, 61–68, 77, 86, 89, 93, 97, 100, 102, 113
definition of, 14–15
development of, 10–13, 17, 22, 32, 33–35
diffuse, 2, 6, 15, 31, 36–51, 53–59, 61, 67, 92
duties of, 7–8, 12, 15, 48
expectations of, 7, 8, 32, 48, 66–69, 83, 90, 113
Federal and State, 65, 84, 98
formal, 2, 3, 16, 77
institutions of, 3, 6, 18, 22, 29–30, 32, 108, 113
See also Bureaucracy; Council; Executive Legislature
minimal, 2, 6, 15, 31, 36–51, 53–59, 61, 64–69, 72–73, 92
quarrels with, 6, 8, 32–33, 66–67, 94, 96–100
as social contract, 10–13
services of, 48, 68–69
theories of, 7–8, 10–19, 31–35, 90, 113
See also Authority; Order
Greece, 10, 12, 21
Grievances, 7, 44
See also Conflicts; Disputes; Quarrels; Government, quarrels with
Groups, corporate, 14, 23–24, 27, 30, 31
descent, 16, 27, 28
See also Descent group
interest, 36
See also Interest
reference, 108
Guests, 47–48
Gulliver, P., 70
Gwembe Tonga, *See* Tonga, Gwembe

Hall, R., 97
Hallpike, C. R. 66
Handsome Lake, 64
Harris, Alfred, 86
Hatanaka, S., 70
Headman, village, 50, 79
Heesterman, J. C., 59, 80–81
Hegel, G., 12
Hennigh, L., 41
Herder, J., 12
Hierarchy, absence of, 5, 28, 32
See also Egalitarianism
administrative, 3, 15
See also Administration
questioning of, 1, 32
recognition of, 2, 3, 98
systems, 28
Hobbes, T., 7, 32, 37, 46
Hocart, A. M., 34–35
Hoebel, E. A., 42
Hostility, 41, 44, 52, 61
See also Conflict; Disputes; Envy; Fighting; Feud; Quarrels; Self-help; Wars
Household, as political units, 2, 20–21, 86

Howell, P. P., 70
Hsu, F., 35–36
Hughes, C., 41
Hunger, 38, 48, 50
Hunting societies, 34
Humanism, African, 105

Identification, social, 103–110
See also Categories
Ideology, 8, 20, 38, 90, 102, 103, 105–106, 110, 112–113
Immigrants, absorption of, 26–27, 28, 29
Independence, personal, 3, 71, 74, 76
political, 2, 7, 36, 62, 67–69, 90, 97–98, 113
See also Freedom
India, 18, 80, 103
Indian Affairs, Bureau of, 2, 42, 84–86
Indians, American, 2, 16, 24, 44–45, 65–66, 84–87, 92
Individualism, 32, 36, 51, 58–59, 95
Indonesia, 80
Inequality, 14, 32–33, 75–76, 110
Innovation, legal and political, 77–87, 92
See also Change; Experimentation
religious, 85–86
See also Church; Religious movements
Institutions, 6, 77, 81
legal, 7, 61, 77, 87, 113
political, 5, 9, 17, 18–19, 75, 78, 83, 87, 92
social, 17, 18, 62–63, 75, 97
Insult, 38, 41, 53, 56
Intellectuals, 7, 102, 105
Interaction, social, 5–6, 19, 30, 57–58, 107–109
Interests, common, 8, 36, 52, 53, 75, 77, 91, 93, 110
conflict of, 8, 14, 52, 100
individual, 4, 46, 52, 53, 77, 110
See also Ambition
Iran, 43, 67
Iroquois, v, xi, 3, 9, 11, 12, 17, 19–30, 41, 63–64
adoption among, 20, 24, 28–29
clans, 16, 19–25, 28–30
Confederacy, 11, 12–13, 19, 24, 29, 63–64
council, 16, 19, 20, 29–30, 41
matrilineality, 12–20
political order, 5, 12–13, 15–16, 19–30, 54, 63–64
warfare, 19, 29
women, 19–20

Jacobson, David, 107–108
Jehovah's Witnesses, 98
Jefferson, Thomas, 9
Jesus Movement, 95
Joking, as social control, 40, 54, 56
Judge, 33, 79
Judgment, 4, 51, 52, 53–59, 69–74, 83, 89, 97–98
enforcement of, 73, 89
See also Adjudication; Courts
Jurisdiction, 2, 73, 97–98
Justice, 8, 87

Kaberry, P., 40, 119
Kampala, city of, 107
Kariba Lake, 68
Kenya, 54
Kimbanguism, 85
Kingdoms, African, 17, 93, 98, 99
Kingship, 10, 17–18, 21, 35, 64, 80, 86

Kinship, 3, 13–14, 20–21, 27, 34, 37, 39, 40, 41, 47–48, 50, 56, 58, 71, 72–73, 89, 98, 109, 111, 112
classificatory, 23, 25–26, 27
Kitawala, 85
Kluckhohn, Clyde, 41–42, 45, 57–58
Kuper, A., 18
Kwakiutl, 16

Lakalai, 40
Latin America, 93
Law, 3, 7, 11, 18, 31–32, 35, 45, 51, 54, 55, 61, 73, 77, 78, 79, 80, 82, 86, 87, 98, 101, 106, 110–112
Blue, 81
codified, 74, 80–81
enforcement, 3, 30–31, 33, 34, 69, 72
promulgation, 3, 7, 31, 79
rule of, 14–15, 18, 31, 32, 42, 51, 54, 77, 96, 111–113
Lawrence, P., 37, 70
Leach, E., 14–15, 92
Leacock, Eleanor, xi
Leaders, African, 7, 8, 67, 82–83, 102, 104–106
political, 7, 8, 27, 73–74, 79, 97–98, 110, 112–113
See also Elites
Leadershp, 3, 27, 33–34, 98
political, 3, 64, 67–69, 74, 79, 83, 90, 97, 102
League of the Iroquois, xi, 10, 15, 22, 23
Legal, institutions, 7, 10, 34, 42, 74
system, 42, 54–59, 69–74
See also Adjudication; Courts; Law; Moot
Legality, as social control, 6, 76, 86–87
Legislation, 3, 11, 18, 77–78, 79–80, 81, 82–83, 84, 87, 111
Legislative bodies, 10, 29–30, 87, 106, 111
See also Assembly; Council
Legitimacy, political, 7, 11, 12, 25, 64, 76
principles, of, 2, 28, 47, 50, 52, 57, 72, 77, 81, 82, 84, 97
Lehmann, D., 96
Lenshina, Alice, 85, 96–98
Leviathan, 32
Levi-Strauss, C., 6
Liability, legal, 42–43
Liberty, v, 7, 32, 62–69
See also Freedom
Life-styles, 6, 105–113
Limits, self-imposed, 4, 19, 30, 106
See also Restraint
Lineage, 27, 39, 70
segmentary, 17, 23, 70
Litigation, 10, 69–74
See also Adjudication; Courts; Disputes; Law; Moot
Locke, John, 7, 9, 10, 12
Long, N., 99
Lowie, R., 16, 17
Loyalty, 24, 103
Lubbock, Sir John, 11
Lugbara, 70
Lumpa Church, 96–98, 101, 112
Luri, 43, 67

McLennan, J. F., 11
Maine, Sir Henry, 5, 11, 17
Mair, Lucy, 2, 15, 31, 61, 94, 95, 104
Makah, ix, 2, 3, 16, 22, 41, 45
Malawi, 27, 78, 98
Malinowski, B., 45–47

Man, nature of, 4, 13, 14, 19, 32–51, 87, 92, 105–106
  perfectibility of, 86–87, 92–96
Marshall, Lorna, 43
Marwick, M., 85
Marx, Karl, 16
Matrilineality, 19–20, 21, 22, 25
Mauss, M., 45
Mbale, town of, 107–108
Medicine, 49, 93–94, 97
Meebelo, Henry, 85, 99, 105
Messiah, 64
Middleton, John, 52, 70
Migration, labor, 82, 107–110
Miller, Frank, 84
Missionaries, 85, 99
Mitchell, Clyde, 104
Mobility, geographical, 7, 8, 57–58, 62, 71, 82, 101, 106–113
  social, 7, 28, 62, 105–113
Model, political or social, 1, 15–19, 23, 24, 25, 26, 30, 35, 108–110
  See also Political, theory; Society, theory of
Mohawk, 23
Moot, 50, 70, 71, 72–73, 80
Moore, Sally F., 36, 42–43
Morgan, Lewis Henry, x, xi, 2, 4, 9–30, 31, 33, 44, 47, 62, 63, 75, 91
  and Iroquois, v, 5, 12, 19–30, 63
  and Political Anthropology, v, 5, 13–19
  and Social Contract, v, 10–13
  and social control, 5
  and study of kinship, 13–14
  Lectures, x, 1, 91
Multiplex society, definition of, 5–6, 72
  See also Community, small-scale
Murdock, G. P., 46, 51
Myth, political, 25, 87, 90

Nader, L., 73
Nationalism, 12, 103
Nature, state of, 32–34
Navaho, 41–42, 45, 57–58
Negotiation, 1, 4, 8, 51, 58, 64, 70, 100
Neighbors, controls by, 7, 53–59, 62, 107–108, 110
  fear of, 6, 32, 42, 48–49, 57–58, 89, 112
Network, kinship, 22
  political, 24
  professional, 106, 107, 108–109
  social, 5, 38, 54–59, 72–73, 74, 102, 106–110
New Guinea, 18, 37–38, 40, 44, 64–65, 68, 69, 70, 73
New York State, 10, 11, 12
Ngoni, 78
Nigeria, 70
Nomads, 43, 67
Northern Rhodesia, 3, 96
  See also Zambia
Nuer, 70
Nyerere, Julius, 105

Obligation, 52–53
Occupation, 103, 106, 107–113
Office, 1, 7, 15, 105–106
  collective, 15
  ritual, 2, 27
  political 2, 5, 27, 28, 31, 77, 104
  public, 4, 7, 15, 36, 76, 77
  See also Chief; Executive; Officials
Officials, colonial,
  public, 2, 4, 6, 7, 10, 33, 62, 64, 69, 76, 77, 82, 89, 93, 94, 96, 103, 106, 113

Officials—*continued*
See also Administration, colonial
Onandaga, 23
Oneida, 23, 29
Order, natural, 93
social, vi, 1, 5, 6, 9, 13, 14, 22, 23, 24, 25, 31, 61, 64, 66, 68–69, 79, 86–87, 89, 92–93, 97, 108, 110–113
development of, 7, 9, 64, 111–113
disillusion with, 1, 75, 102
institution of new, 7–8, 13, 64–65, 96–102, 110–111
maintenance of, 5, 18, 38, 41, 45–47, 61, 68–69, 70–75, 89–90, 93, 106, 110–111
Origin of the State, 17
Organization, principles of, 6, 30, 45–56, 78, 108
purpose of, 30, 53, 86

Panchayat, village, 80
Parliament, 35
Parochialism, 8, 66, 103
Parker, Eli, 12
Parkin, D., 107
Parsons, Elsie Clews, 58
Pastoralists, 57–58
Patriarchy, 21–22
Patrol officers, in New Guinea, 38, 64–65
Patronage, 79
Peace, 12, 13, 32, 33, 37, 40, 43, 46, 62–69, 89, 90, 94, 113
peacemaking, 46
See also Order
Peers, 4, 55, 58–59
Penalties, 46–47, 53–59
See also Punishment; Sanctions
Person, total, 53–59, 90
Peters, E., 54–55
Peyote Church, 86
Planning, 19, 62, 91
Plateau Tonga, *See* Tonga, Plateau
Police, 4, 42, 62, 64, 72, 110
power, 3, 64–69
Policy, political, 13, 14, 18, 30, 37, 74, 77, 78, 79, 110
Political, action, 14–15, 19
anthropology, v, ix, 5, 11, 13–19, 31, 75
competition, 14–15, 69, 79
definition of, 14–15
development, 19, 20
fields, 15, 18
ideology, *See* Ideology
institutions, 5, 18, 43, 75, 78
leaders, *See* Leaders, political
movements, 68, 85, 96–98
offices, *See* Office
parties, 18, 69, 76, 79, 83, 96–98, 101
processes, 18–19, 81, 82
resources, 15, 18
Science, 14, 31
strategies, 15, 79, 82
systems, 13, 15–19
theory, 4, 5, 9–19, 20, 23, 31–34, 105–106
units, 2, 3, 5, 18, 21, 22, 28, 107, 113
Politics, 8, 18, 78, 103–109
Polity, 2, 3, 8, 16, 36, 70
clan-based, 5
Pomo, ix, 2, 3, 22, 40–41
Pospisil, L., 92
Power, v, 3, 4, 7, 15, 17–20, 33, 39, 45, 50, 64, 74, 87, 97, 100, 112–113
appropriation of, 7, 8, 19, 29, 59, 68–69, 79
balance of, 28, 59, 64–67
bases of, 7, 79, 100
checks on, 75–87, 90

Power—*continued*
politics of, 8
resistance to, 75–87
struggle for, 32, 83
transfer of, 68
Precedents, 79, 80
Predictability, importance of, 53–59, 63–64, 102–103
See also Expectation
Price, T., 85
Priest, 33
Process, social, 9, 61, 77, 81, 82
Property, 32, 34, 38, 43–45, 67, 69, 72, 110
Protection, legal, 39, 86
self, 48–51
See also Self-help
Public, affairs, 5, 9
goals, 15, 19
interest, 15, 36, 51, 53–59, 61, 76, 94
See also Interest, common
office, *See,* Office
opinion, 33, 51–59, 71, 74, 79, 83
Pueblo Indians, 58
Punishment, 42, 53, 54, 55
See also Sanctions
Purification, 93–95

Quarrels, 38–51, 61, 70, 91, 96
avoidance of, 39, 96
See also Disputes; Fighting

Radcliffe-Brown, A. R., 14, 17, 53
Raid, 38, 65
Ralston, L., 40
Rank, 2, 41
Rebellion, 82, 92–93
Reciprocity, v, 45–51, 72–73
Reconciliation, by court, 73, 79
See also Adjudication; Arbitration
Reform, individual, 56, 91–95
social, 11, 19, 29, 63–64, 73–74, 90, 91–113
Regimes, political, 11, 75, 76, 96–98, 101
Relationships, social, continuity of, 5, 51, 74, 107–109
Religion, 11, 19, 26, 53, 63–64, 74, 78, 85–86, 107, 110
See also Ritual
Religious movements, 2, 19, 63, 64, 85–86, 96–98
Representation, 27, 29–30
See also Assembly; Council
Reputation, importance of, 6, 53–59, 71, 93, 107–108, 111
Resek, C., 9, 10, 11
Reservation, Indian, 2, 84, 86
Resistance, political, 13, 67–69, 75–87, 89, 97–98
Resources, political, 15
sharing of, 37, 52–53, 93
Responsibility, legal, 72–73
Restraint, personal, 6, 37–51, 58, 61, 89, 96, 107, 111
Revenge, 38, 41, 49, 56, 66
See also Feud; Self-help; Vengeance; Retaliation
Revitalization movement, *See* Religious movements
Revolution, 13, 92–93, 102
Rewards, 46–47
Rhodes-Livingstone Institute, x, 23
Rhodesia, Northern, *See* Northern Rhodesia
Richards, A., 18, 85
Ridicule, 40, 56
Rights, constitutional, 84–87
personal, 3, 7, 13, 35, 36, 42, 52, 74–87, 100
to worship, 85, 86, 100

Ritual, offices of, 2, 18
  and conflict, 52, 63, 91–95
  importance of, 34, 91
  and reform, 91–92, 94–95
Roberts, A., 96
Roles, 6, 7, 17, 32, 34, 53, 91, 104, 113
Rome, 10, 12, 21
Rotberg, R., 91
Rousseau, J., 3, 7, 32, 33, 37
Rulers, 5, 6, 8, 17, 21, 28, 64, 74–75, 78, 93, 96–97
Rules, v, 6, 18, 30, 31, 32, 52, 69, 70, 76, 77, 79, 86–87, 95–98
  conflict in, 52
  infraction of, 31
  invention of, 76–79, 80, 102
  normative, 51, 79–80
  utility of, 6, 61–87

Sacrilege, 78
Safety, personal, *See* Security, personal
Sahlins, M., 45–46, 48
Sanctions, 10, 42, 43
  application of, 53–59, 108–109
  religious, 13, 53–59, 78, 108–109
  See also Exile; Joking; Law; Ostracism; Ridicule; Death penalty; Punishment
Sangree, W., 54, 67, 77
Schwartz, T., 92
Scudder, T., ix, x, 63, 68, 109
Secret societies, 2
Security, personal, 6, 8, 32, 34, 45, 59, 66, 67, 74, 75, 88, 89, 110–111
  search for, 6, 64–67, 93–94, 97–98, 110–111
Segmentary political systems, 13, 17, 19, 23, 36, 43, 70
Self-help, 32, 36–51, 53–54, 70, 72, 89, 110
  See also Feud; Vengeance
Seneca, 23, 28
Settlers, 65–66
Shack, W., x, 10, 74, 87
Shaker Church, 86
Sharing, 45–51
  See also Reciprocity
Shepperson, G., 85
Simon, H., 26
Slavery, 38, 42
Social, category, *See* Category
  contract, *See* Contract, Social
  control, *See* Control
  field, 6
  institutions, *See* Institutions
  order, *See* Order
  system, 17, 63, 81
Social Contract, The, 32
Socialism, African, 105
Society, basis of, 45–46
  conflict in, 52–53
  egalitarian, 3, 4, 31–59, 61–62, 66, 69, 70, 89, 90, 92
  face-to-face, 4, 80, 102
    See also Community
  large-scale, 6, 93
  models of, 5, 10, 19, 24–25, 30, 31–35, 45, 46, 90, 92, 93, 95, 100, 102, 105–113
  multiplex, 5–6
  secret, 2
  stateless, 2, 5, 31, 32, 36–51, 53–59, 62–63
Socio-linguists, 6
Solidarity, mechanical, 23
Sorcery, *See* Witchcraft
Sorrenson, E. R., 64–65
Southall, A., 64
Southwold, M., 28
Spencer, Herbert, 33
Spencer, Robert, 41

Stability, political, 18
Standards, v, 43, 51, 52–59, 83, 93, 105, 108
  See also Rules
State, 31–32, 45–46, 66, 89
  centralized, 7, 27, 62–63, 66
  definition, 14–15
  officials, *See* Officials; Executive; Administration
  origin of, 4, 11, 14, 46
  power of, 4, 27, 67, 103
    See also Power
Stern, B., 11
Stranger, dangers from, 38
  incorporation of, 24, 26–28, 105
  treatment of, 70, 71, 105
Strategies, political, 15, 18–19, 24, 82
Structuralists, 6
Structures, social, 6, 18, 30, 32, 113
  questioning of, 1, 32, 66–67
  See also Society
Struggle, political, 79, 83
  See also Political
Sudan, 70
Suspicion, 55–59, 85, 94
  See also Fear
Swartz, M., 15, 24
Symbol, religious, 53
  system, 81

Taboos, food, 49
Tanzania, 70
Taylor, John, 96
Technology, and political development, 14, 16, 18, 34
Territorial units, 3, 14
Theocracy, 17
Theory, political, *See* Political; Society
Thomas, Elizabeth Marshall, 44
Thompson, W. I., 90
Threats, 45, 64, 70
Tiriki, 54
Tiv, 70
Tolerance, 37, 112–113
Tonga, ix, 3–4, 26–28, 38–39, 41, 44, 47–51, 53, 55–56, 59, 62–63, 70–73, 86, 94–95, 104–105
  Gwembe, ix, 3, 38, 44, 47–51, 67–69, 71–73, 94–95, 109
  Plateau, ix, 38
Totems, 24, 26
Trade union, 83
Tradition, v, 7, 11, 35, 73, 90, 103, 105–106, 111
  as social control, 6, 35, 74–87, 89, 111
  as legislation, 18, 77–78, 84, 87
Treaty rights, 65, 84
Trial, 54–59, 72–73
  See also Ajudication; Courts; Moot
Tribalism, 103–105
Trobriands, 47
Trouble-maker, 41, 53, 68
Tuden, A., 15
Turner, V., 15, 52, 79, 91
Tuscorora, 29
Tylor, Sir Edward, 11
Tyranny, 67, 77

Uganda, 64, 70, 106–108
Unilineal descent groups, 16
  See also Descent
United States, 10, 11, 12, 16, 83–87, 95, 98, 103
  and tradition, 83–87
Urbanization, 82
  See also City
Utopia, vi, 8, 89, 92, 111, 113
  blueprint for, 1, 8, 102, 113
  dreams of, v, 90, 94, 96–102, 111

Utopia—*continued*
search for, 89–113
Utilitarianism, 46

Valley Tonga, *See* Tonga, Gwembe
Values, 62–63, 66–67, 82, 105–108, 111–113
Van Velsen, J., 73, 124
Venezuela, 66
Vengeance, 12, 24
See also Feud; Self-help; Revenge
Vincent, Joan, 106–107
Violence, 7, 8, 13, 14, 37–51, 89, 110, 111
control of, 14, 36–51, 69
See also Control, social

Wales, 54–55
Wallace, A., 12–13, 19, 28–29, 55, 63
Wallis, W., 64
Warfare, 24, 29, 37–38, 64–66
effect on political development, 19, 33, 37, 64–69
Watchtower Church, 88–100, 101, 112
Wealth, 2, 14, 18, 38, 44
See also Property
Weber, Max, 76
Werbner, R., 80
Williams, Nancy, 40
Wilson, Godfrey, 62, 66
Wilson, Monica, 59, 62, 66
Witch, 38, 39, 45, 50, 51, 56, 57–59, 93, 96–97, 101
Witchcraft, 38, 42, 43, 48–51, 54, 56–59, 63, 93–97, 112
Witch-finding movements, 93–97, 100–101, 112
Women, Church of, 85
See also Lumpa Church
Women, exchange of, 22
role of Iroquois women, 20–22
Woodcock, G., 32
Work party, 55

Yalman, Nur, 76
Yạnomamö, 66

Zaire, 27, 64
Zambia, ix, x, 3, 26–27, 38, 39, 62, 67, 68, 70, 73, 78, 94, 96–98, 109
Ziff, L., 95
Zulu, J. B., 105
Zuni, 58

TRADITION AND CONTRACT
The Problem of Order
Elizabeth Colson

Publisher / Alexander J. Morin
Production Editor / Georganne E. Marsh
Production Manager / Mitzi Carole Trout

Composition by Typoservice Corp.,
Indianapolis, Indiana
Printed by Printing Headquarters, Inc.,
Arlington Heights, Illinois
Bound by Brock & Rankin, Chicago, Illinois